BREW FOOD

GREAT BEER-INSPIRED APPETIZERS, MAIN COURSES, AND DESSERTS

Foreword © 2012 by Brandon Hernández
Tempeh Shepherd's Pie with Stone IPA Garlicky Mashed Potatoes recipe by Alex Carballo, Chief Culinary Philosopher,
Stone Brewing World Bistro & Gardens, was used with permission. Originally published in "The Craft of Stone Brewing Co."
© 2011 by Ten Speed Press, Berkeley, California.

Published by Chefs Press, Inc., San Diego, California
www.chefspress.com

Publisher: Amy Stirnkorb
President & CEO: Bruce Glassman
Executive Vice President: Michael D. Pawlenty
Photographs: Michael D. Pawlenty
Proofreader: Margaret King

On the Cover: At The Marine Room in La Jolla, California, a glass of Lightning Brewery's Thunderweizen sits alongside Chef Ron Oliver's Hefeweizen Coriander-Baked Sea Bass in a Tangerine-Scented Reduction with Fresh Corn and Tomato.

Special Thanks: The Publisher would like to give special thanks to Melody Daversa from Karl Strauss Brewing Company for all her help in collecting material for this project. Hearty thanks also go to Randy Clemens from Stone Brewing Co. for his invaluable assistance behind the scenes, as well as his considerable talents in front-of-the-scenes. Big thanks to Brian Malarkey, who helped to coordinate recipes from some of his great restaurants, and an extra thanks to Peter Zien of AleSmith Brewing Company, for his guidance and expertise along the way.

ISBN-13: 978-0-9816222-6-2

First Edition
Printed in China

BREW FOOD

GREAT BEER-INSPIRED APPETIZERS, MAIN COURSES, AND DESSERTS

TEXT BY BRUCE GLASSMAN
PHOTOGRAPHY BY MIKE PAWLENTY
FOREWORD BY BRANDON HERNÁNDEZ

Chefs Press, Inc.
San Diego, California

inside

starters | sides

Sculpin Beer Cheese **14**
Toronado's Famous Fromage Fort **17**
Lil' Devil Salad with Lil' Devil Poached Shrimp and Vinaigrette **18**
Company Pub's Carrot and Orange Soup **21**
Alesmith's Wee Heavy Artisan Bread **22**
Roasted Apple Soup with Hoppy "Grilled Cheese" **25**
The Chicks for Beer Chica Fresca Shrimp Ceviche **29**
Classic San Diego Fish Tacos with Chipotle Lime Cole Slaw **30**
Cauliflower, Beer, and Gruyere Soup **33**
Crab-Stuffed Wontons in Manzanita Blonde Creamy Tomato Sauce **34**
Stone's Tilapia Ceviche **37**
Beer Cheese Soup with Black Forest Bacon and Parmesan Garlic Croutons **38**
Wasabi Cole Slaw **40**
Spicy-O-Life BBQ Basting or Dipping Sauce **41**
Long Beans Topped with a Fried Egg **43**
Burgers and Dogs Surf & Turf: Chorizo Turkey Slider, Roasted Pepper Chili, Spicy Pickle Chip
and Smoked Gouda Biscuit with Shrimp Sausage and Crawfish Etouffée **44**
***Pairing Beer and Cheese: Ideas and Inspirations* 48**

main courses

Wahoo Wheat Cioppino **60**

Judgment Day Steamed Carlsbad Mussels with Andouille Sausage, Eggplant, and Mushrooms **63**

Green Flash Barleywine-Glazed Salmon **64**

Small Bar's Beer-Batter Fish with Remoulade **66**

Brown Butter-Seared Scallops with IPA Gastrique, Hop Flower Dust, and Candied Peanuts **69**

Steamed Black Cod with Maitake Mushrooms and Manila Clams in AleSmith Horny Devil Nage **71**

Ginger Mussels and Sour Wench **75**

Hefeweizen Coriander-Baked Sea Bass in a Tangerine-Scented Reduction with Fresh Corn and Tomato **76**

Brewmaster's Beer-Battered Fish Tacos **78**

Hess Brewing's Grazias Para Paella **80**

Cali Belgique Braised Pork with Orange and Fennel over Jasmine Rice **82**

Creole Eggs in Purgatory with Hop Butter-Fried Eggs, Jambalaya Risotto Cakes, Crawfish, Sauce Piquánt and Worcestershire Porter Reduction **84**

Bunz Burger with Smoked Porter Bacon Jam **88**

Toronado's Arrabiata (Arra·beer·ata) **91**

Gingham's Beer-Braised Lamb Shanks **92**

Tiger! Tiger! Bratwurst **94**

Three Li'l Pigs Burger (Pulled Pork, Bacon, and Ham with Beer-Thyme Mustard) **96**

Pork Stout Osso Buco **98**

Velvet Glove Mac 'n' Cheese **100**

Sour Wench-Braised Duck with Smashed Savory Yams and Garlicky Greens **103**

Lightning Pulled Pork Sandwiches with Sweet-and-Sour Cole Slaw **105**

Chris Gort's Brewer's Flatbread Pizza & Pizza with Bacon & Sour Cream Topping **108**

Cowboy Chicken Sandwich with Beer-Batter Onion Rings and Stone Smoked Porter BBQ Sauce **110**

Urge Gastropub's Sculpin Mac & Cheese **113**

Spicy Curry with Crispy Pork Belly and Hop Oil **114**

Searsucker's Cali Belgique Short Rib Sandwich with Horseradish Sauce **116**

Cinnamon-Dusted Pork Tenderloin with Jalapeño-Yam Hash, Cilantro Pesto and Chocolate Stout Mole **118**

Tempeh Shepherd's Pie with Stone IPA Garlicky Mashed Potatoes **122**

Three-Day Mission Amber Pork Belly (aka "Beer Belly") **124**

Easy Aztec Beer Mac & Cheeze **126**

Stout-Braised Pork Belly with Cocoa Crust and Red Beet Slaw **129**

Spicy IPA Burger with IPA Onion Strings and Apricot Habanero Ketchup **131**

Stone Smoked Porter Chili **134**

BBQ'd Jerked Barleywine Chicken with Succotash **136**

Mission Amber Ale Braised Short Ribs **138**

Coq Au Bier **140**

Quad-Braised Osso Buco **142**

Paul Segura's Favorite Big Beer Burger with Beer Onions and Beer-Brined Bacon **145**

Chef Gunther's Pot Roast Sliders with Black Garlic-Truffle Horseradish Sauce **147**

Goulash and Dumplings **150**

Sweet Georgia Brown Lamb Stew on Roasted Garlic Mashed Potatoes **152**

Imperial Stout Pot Roast **155**

Ritual's Perfect Pork Belly with Glazed Carrots and Parsnip Purée **156**

Matt Rattner's Favorite BBQ Carnitas Pizza **158**

Avant Garde Herb-Crusted Lamb Medallions with Avant Garde Whipped Potatoes **161**

***Hosting Your Own Beer Dinner: Ideas and Inspirations* 164**

San Diego Crostini With Elder Flower Cream Cheese, Sage Pesto, and Local Smoked Yellowtail **168**

Chile Wahoo Wheat Mixta Ceviche on Duck-Fat Tortillas **171**

Grilled Lamb Chops with Puréed Parsnips, Glazed Carrots, and Blackberry Sauce **173**

Orange Sculpin Cake with Orange-Mango Semifreddo **176**

Chocolate and Goat Cheese with a Balsamic Black Marlin Reduction **179**

breakfast | desserts

Oatmeal Stout-and-Bacon Belgian Waffles **182**
Searsucker's Apple & Ale Muffins **185**
Navigator Dopplebock Bread Pudding with Rum Raisin Caramel and Blue Cheese Whipped Cream **186**
Grand Cru Strawberry and Kumquat Galette **188**
Toronado's Stout Nutella Trifle **191**
Chocolate and Stout Pot de Crème with Malt Florentine Cookies **192**
Black Marlin Cake with Cocoa Malt Ice Cream and Raspberry Coulis **194**
Rock Bottom Stout Cupcakes **196**
High Dive Wahoo Lemon Bars **199**
Older Viscosity Stout Cake with Whipped Cream and Ganache Glaze **200**
Mother Earth Mancakes with Vanilla Cream Ale Frosting **203**
No Judgment Here Goat Cheese and Raspberry Cheesecake with Beer Caramel and Fresh Berries **204**
Chris Cramer's Favorite Imperial Stout Crème Brûlée **206**
Green Tea Layer Cake with Beer Frosting Two Ways **208**
Russian Imperial Beer Nog **211**

resources **212** | index **215** | beer index **220**

foreword

BY BRANDON HERNÁNDEZ

This book comes to you from a city and county that lives, eats, breathes, and DRINKS great craft beer. San Diego has long enjoyed its reputation as the craft brewing capital of the United States. Over the past two-plus decades, beer has grown into an integral element that has unified diverse communities all across San Diego county. Today, "America's Finest City" is home to well over 50 brewhouses, all working to produce exquisite handcrafted ales and lagers. Many San Diego breweries have garnered national and international praise and have won many awards.

It's only fitting that a book dedicated entirely to cooking with (and of course drinking) craft beer should spring from this environment. Whether you're taking in the sun-kissed shores of coastal bergs, sightseeing downtown, or venturing out for a day-trip to the mountain town of Julian, craft beer is never out of reach in San Diego. It has seeped into — and saturated — every square mile of territory and has won the hearts, minds, and palates of San Diego's people.

The craft beer culture reflected in the pages and recipes of this book is as rich, full-bodied, and multi-layered as a bourbon barrel-aged barleywine. The county is a hotbed of brew-and-food activity that features beer-pairing dinners, brewmaster banquets, brewery-and-food-truck collaborations, as well as full-scale festivals that happen on a near weekly basis. Add to that an ever-growing legion of brewpubs, gastropubs, and beer-centric eateries and you have one vibrant and unique SoCal suds scene.

As that scene has matured, and the prominence of the brewing subculture has skyrocketed, San Diego's culinary community has embraced the wealth of great beer options available — first as an enjoyable choice for off-hour imbibing and, more recently, as an exciting medium for culinary experimentation. In San Diego, craft beers are no longer regarded solely as accompaniments to great cuisine, they are actually ingredients that are capable of elevating the flavor of all kinds of dishes, from classic comfort food to the avant-garde.

Even chefs at restaurants without a beery emphasis have begun to utilize beers to enhance their recipes. It's not uncommon to find menus using all kinds of brews — everything from piney IPAs to fruity Belgian quads to theobromine imperial stouts. Chefs are using beer as the backbone for sauces, marinades, purées, and braising liquids and are relying on it to add extra flavors to creative condiments, accouterments, and garnishes. They have discovered — as you will in reading this book — that the ways in which beer can be utilized in the kitchen are practically limitless.

This is what *Brew Food* celebrates — the incredible range and versatility of quality beer and its adaptability to the home kitchen. The recipes in this book have been culled from a multifarious assemblage of professionals, each deeply entrenched in the beer and food industry. The book highlights the culinary creativity of chefs and dessertiers, pro brewers, brewery staffers, bar and restaurant owners, and even one very honored beer-and-food journalist.

The common denominator for all the book's contributors is an abiding love for craft beer and its use in the culinary arts, as well as an enthusiasm for sharing the joys of this "new frontier" of cookery.

For home cooks looking to try their hand at gourmet preparations, there are dishes like roasted apple soup with hop-scented *queso fresco* from the likes of Kyle Bergman, chef at The Lodge at Torrey Pines, or a baked sea bass with a tangerine-and-hefeweizen reduction from chef Ron Oliver of The Marine Room at La Jolla Shores.

Other high profile, beer-loving chefs from some of San Diego's trendiest restaurants have offered up their talents and techniques for this book as well. Katherine Humphus, the youthful up-and-comer behind the French bistro Bo-Beau Kitchen + Bar, created a dish of seared scallops with hop flower dust and an IPA gastrique specifically for this project. Others, such as Ryan Studebaker, chef at Gingham (one of the area's highly popular "Brian Malarkey hotspots") offered up his recipe for beer-braised lamb shanks. Dessert maven and pastry chef Rachel King developed a special recipe for "apple and ale" muffins that get their character from fresh Galas and a few glugs of great nut brown. Sweets innovator Misty Birchall, whose entire business is built around gourmet beer cupcakes, has also come through with a few gems. Typically, the recipes for PubCakes are off limits, but she's given us a malted milk chocolate and English-style porter cupcake that would normally be locked in her recipe vault and guarded by Pinkertons somewhere.

From the beginning, the goal of this book was to offer a wide variety of recipes that encompass all kinds

Brandon Hernández

of food and skill levels. Just as a craft beer fan can choose the level of exploration that's comfortable, so can the user of *Brew Food*. From some of San Diego's most popular gastropubs come some of San Diego's most satisfying beer dishes. Chef Aaron LaMonica, of the urban chic craft beer hubs Blind Lady Ale House and Tiger! Tiger! Tavern, shares his method for making bratwursts from scratch. Macaroni and cheese is made extra decadent with the addition of a tropical IPA by Urge Gastropub chef Marc Liautard. A plate of braised pork belly cooked like a duck confit in beer

Toronado's Stout Nutella Trifle

Ballast Point Sour Wench-Braised Duck

is made even more "perfect" with soy-and-brown-ale-glazed carrots, a recipe from Ritual Tavern's chef Adrian Ramirez.

As San Diego's beerophile-geared dining options continue to grow, its best craft beer bars are raising their game, adding full menus that go far beyond the standard onion rings and chicken tenders. Leading that charge are Tyson Blake from O'Brien's Pub (a bar known around the nation as "the hoppiest place on Earth") and Nate Soroko, the chef at the bustling beer haven, Toronado. Nate gave us recipes for a beer pasta sauce, a baked beer cheese, and an incredible trifle made with Nutella and stout.

No San Diego beer cookbook would be complete without contributions from long-time beer-and-food innovators like chef Gunther Emathinger from Karl Strauss Brewing Company. In 1989, Karl Strauss

opened the city's first new brewpub since the repeal of Prohibition. The company is now six brewery restaurants strong, focusing not only on beer-and-food pairings, but on the creation of hundreds of dishes that use beer as a key ingredient. Gunther was kind enough to share his recipes for pot roast sliders with a sauce made from black garlic, horseradish, and truffle oil; his IPA burger, his carnitas pizza, and one of his most decadent sweet treats: his imperial stout crème brûlée.

Brew Food was also fortunate to receive great contributions from another San Diego brewing icon — Stone Brewing Co. Chef Alex Carballo, from Stone Brewing World Bistro and Gardens, contributed his recipes for tilapia ceviche and a vegan shepherd's pie made with tempeh and IPA-infused mashed potatoes. He's joined by a number of his esteemed colleagues, including brewmaster Mitch Steele, cicerone "Dr."

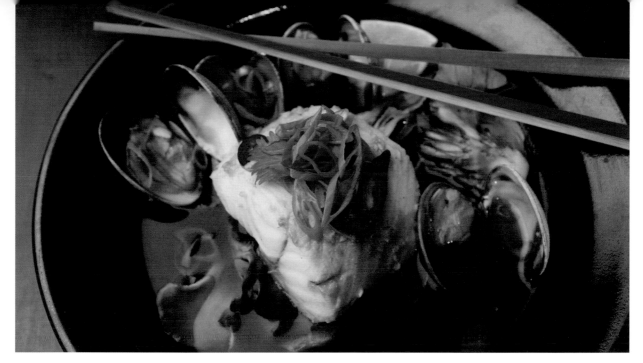

Steamed Black Cod with Maitake Mushrooms and Manila Clams in AleSmith Horny Devil Nage

Bill Sysak, and media linchpin Randy Clemens, all of whom graciously shared some of their favorite beer-inspired recipes for this project.

The true worth of *Brew Food* lies in the variety of options within its pages. Unlike cookbooks that focus on niche subjects, such as cooking with a particular protein, mastering an individual piece of kitchen equipment, or studying a singular culture's gastronomic heritage, this book was built to provide the basis for culinary fun and exploration. It is our hope that it will appeal to people of all walks of life and all levels of culinary skill or interest.

Cutting-edge haute cuisine, pub grub, ethnic dishes, and family recipes that have been passed down for generations — all of this and more is represented on these pages. *Brew Food* truly embodies the love and enthusiasm San Diegans bring to the creation

and enjoyment of craft beer. And, in the spirit of loving craft beer, this book brings together an array of individuals, ideologies, ingredients, and recipes, all of which flavor San Diegans' way of life and, more succinctly, their approach to elevating beer to its proper, lofty place in the culinary world. Cheers and *bon appetit*!

Brandon Hernández is a native San Diegan and an award-winning freelance beer-and-food journalist. He is an editor for the Zagat Survey, the San Diego correspondent for Celebrator Beer News *and a columnist for regionally-based publications* San Diego Magazine, The San Diego Reader *and* West Coaster. *He has been a consultant for Food Network and is a frequent contributor to national publications including* Imbibe, The Beer Connoisseur, Beer West, Beer Magazine *and* Wine Enthusiast. *To keep up with his stories on food, beer, restaurants and the craft brewing industry, follow him on Twitter at @offdutyfoodie or check out his official website —* www.thebrandonhernandez.com.

starters | sides

SCULPIN BEER CHEESE

JACK & JENNIFER WHITE, OWNERS, BALLAST POINT BREWING & SPIRITS [serves 8–10]

"*The inspiration for this recipe really comes from my mother-in-law,*" explains Jack White, owner and founder of Ballast Point Brewing & Spirits. Jack notes that Barbara Graham, his wife Jennifer's mother, "*really loves experimenting with all our beers — she has done a million different recipes, from desserts to main courses to all kinds of beer cheeses, and now she's handed the mantel over to Jen, who has put her own twist on it.*"

2 cloves garlic
¾ cup Ballast Point Sculpin Beer
3 cups cheddar cheese, grated
1 cup cream cheese, cubed
1 teaspoon mustard powder
1 teaspoon freshly ground black pepper
¼ teaspoon cayenne
¼ teaspoon creamy horseradish
Crackers, for serving
Toasted baguette slices, for serving

[PREPARATION]
1. With a food processor running, drop the garlic through the feed tube and continue to run for 30 seconds. Stop.
2. Add remaining ingredients. Run the food processor until all the ingredients are well blended.
3. Chill for at least 2 hours. Serve with crackers or baguette slices.

PERFECT PAIRING

SCULPIN IPA is the obvious perfect pairing for the richness and creaminess of this recipe. Any other great IPA or Pale Ale would certainly do the trick as well. Be careful: once you start eating this cheese and pairing it with beer, it's hard to stop!

Jennifer White: "I've tried to create this dish so you really taste the beer in it. A lot of time beer cheese is overwhelmed by all the flavors and spices you put into it, but in this version, you can taste the Sculpin. That's why this recipe is a favorite."

TORONADO'S FAMOUS FROMAGE FORT

NATE SOROKO, HEAD CHEF, TORONADO SAN DIEGO   *[serves 4]*

½ cup smoked cheddar cheese, shredded
½ cup cream cheese
½ cup goat cheese
1 tablespoon Dijon mustard
3 cloves garlic, crushed
1 bunch fresh parsley
1 large shallot
5 ounces bacon bits, optional
6 ounces guezue (I use Fond Tradition) or tart beer
1 to 3 tablespoons olive oil
Salt and pepper, to taste
Toasted baguette slices, for serving
Good salami slices, for serving
Fresh blackberries and blueberries, for serving

Beer?

[PREPARATION]

1. Allow cheeses to come to room temperature. Place the cheeses in a food processor along with mustard, garlic, parsley, shallot, and bacon, if using. Purée the mixture for 1 to 2 minutes, until combined.
2. Add the beer and olive oil, and blend until mixture is smooth. Season with salt and pepper to taste.
3. Serve immediately with baguette slices, salami, or berries. (Note: if not serving right away, tightly wrap and refrigerate. Allow to warm to room temperature before serving.)

"I used to make fromage fort *(French for "strong cheese") at another restaurant, but it was a traditional recipe, with white wine, a chardonnay," Nate explains. "I've also done beer cheeses but usually those are done with a maltier beer." Nate says that the flavor profiles of chardonnay and guezue beer are very similar, so he thought of substituting one for the other in this recipe. "Usually when people come into Toronado and want a white wine, I give them a little guezue or sour (beer) to taste."*

This dish will stand up to a wide range of beers and flavors, everything from light, crisp, palate-refreshing pilsners to hoppy pale ales and IPAs — all the way through the sour beers. Acidity to cut through the fattiness of the cheese is the key strategy here.

PERFECT PAIRING

LIL' DEVIL SALAD
WITH LIL' DEVIL POACHED SHRIMP AND VINAIGRETTE

TYSON BLAKE, GENERAL MANAGER, O'BRIEN'S PUB

[serves 4]

Tyson Blake created this appetizer/salad recipe years ago while developing the menu for an AleSmith beer dinner. "Lil' Devil is one of those beers that has delicious coriander and citrus peel flavors," Tyson says. "It's real bright and light, so I always thought it was perfect for pairing with seafood." Once the ale starts cooking, he says, it also takes on a "distinctive winey note, which is like what you'd see in a classic court bouillon (fish poaching liquid)."

For the vinaigrette:
1 shallot, finely diced
1 serrano pepper, seeded, membrane removed, and finely diced*
5 cloves garlic, chopped
2 tablespoons champagne vinegar
2 cups plus 2 tablespoons AleSmith Lil' Devil (or Belgian golden ale or white ale)
1 tablespoon Dijon mustard
½ to ⅓ cup olive oil
½ bunch cilantro, chopped
Salt and pepper, to taste

For the shrimp:
1 cup vegetable stock
¼ pound unsalted butter
1 small yellow onion, chopped
1 teaspoon coriander seeds
1 tablespoon granulated sugar
1 navel orange or mandarin orange, zested
1 clove garlic, finely diced
1 pound 10–12 count shrimp, deveined and peeled, tails on

continued >

PERFECT PAIRING

Tyson says the perfect pairing for this dish is a beer that's effervescent and crisp. "Look for a Belgian pale ale or a blonde ale, something that's not too hoppy and is on the light end and dry end." **ALESMITH'S X** and **IRON FIST'S RENEGADE BLONDE** are two great examples.

For the greens:

2 bunches spinach or arugula, rinsed and dried

2 mandarin oranges or navel oranges, peeled, seeded, and segmented

1 small jicama, peeled and cut into matchstick-size pieces

1 small beet, peeled and cut into matchsticks

½ red onion, thinly sliced

[PREPARATION]

1. Make the vinaigrette: Whisk together the shallot, serrano pepper, garlic, champagne vinegar, and 2 tablespoons of the Lil' Devil in a mixing bowl. Let stand for 5 minutes. Add the mustard and slowly drizzle in the olive oil while whisking constantly. Stir in ¼ cup of the cilantro, season with salt and pepper, and set aside.

2. Cook the shrimp: Combine the stock, butter, yellow onion, coriander seeds, sugar, orange zest, garlic, and the remaining beer in a small saucepan over medium heat. Season with salt and pepper and bring to a simmer. Reduce heat to medium-low and add the shrimp. Cook, gently stirring, for 5 minutes. Remove the shrimp and let cool slightly while you assemble the salad.

3. Prepare the greens: Combine the greens, oranges, jicama, beet, red onion, and the remaining cilantro in a small bowl. Drizzle the mixture with about 4 tablespoons of the vinaigrette and lightly toss. Place a bit of the salad in the middle of each plate, top with shrimp, and lightly drizzle with additional vinaigrette. Serve immediately.

Note: Wear gloves when dicing peppers, and avoid touching your eyes.

Peter Green: "Our twist on this soup is to replace the traditional chicken stock with orange wheat beer. We love the simplicity and the fact that it's a lower-calorie and lower-sodium version of the traditional vegetable soup."

COMPANY PUB'S CARROT AND ORANGE SOUP

PETER GREEN, OWNER, COMPANY PUB AND KITCHEN

[serves 2-4]

1 tablespoon olive oil
⅓ stick butter
1 medium yellow onion, chopped
1 clove garlic, crushed
12 ounces orange wheat beer
  (I like Hangar 24)
1 medium potato, peeled and
  chopped
1 pound carrots, peeled and sliced

1 cup freshly squeezed
  orange juice
¼ cup buttermilk
¼ cup plain yogurt
1 teaspoon honey
¼ teaspoon white pepper
Optional spices: Ginger, cayenne,
  basil, cilantro, parsley, nutmeg,
  cinnamon

[PREPARATION]

1. In a medium stockpot, heat the olive oil over medium heat and melt the butter. Add the onion and sauté for 1 to 2 minutes. Stir in the garlic.
2. When the onions are translucent, slowly add the beer and bring to a boil. Add the potato and carrots, and reduce heat to medium. Add orange juice and stir. Simmer for 20 to 30 minutes, until the carrots and potatoes are very soft. Blend or purée with an immersion blender until the mixture is smooth.
3. In a small bowl, combine the buttermilk, yogurt, honey, and white pepper, and add to the stockpot slowly while stirring.
4. Adjust seasonings. Taste and add more beer or orange juice if desired. You can also add a pinch of any of the optional spices.
5. Simmer over medium heat until ready to serve.

Peter Green has been in the pub business for quite some time. He has always believed the axiom that you can judge a restaurant first and foremost by its soup, so he set out to create a delicious signature soup for his Company Pub. Peter also likes the fact that this recipe highlights the great local produce he can get in Southern California. And as a pub owner, he is happy that the recipe highlights beer.

A variety of wheat beers would complement this soup, including **HANGAR 24 ORANGE WHEAT, CORONADO'S ORANGE AVENUE WIT**, or **LIGHTNING'S THUNDERWEIZEN. IRON FIST'S SPICE OF LIFE** (Belgian-style ale) is made with orange peel and would go beautifully with this soup.

PERFECT PAIRING

ALESMITH'S WEE HEAVY ARTISAN BREAD

PETER ZIEN, OWNER, ALESMITH BREWING CO.

[makes 1 large round loaf]

Beer-making is a process that takes weeks, notes AleSmith owner Peter Zien. Because of that, he says, "I look for more instant gratification, like breadmaking. I like to make this bread with the same ingredients we use in our beer."

Chef's Notes: *This recipe is made in two steps, so start it the day before you want to bake. Step 1: Poolish (starter dough), sits overnight. Step 2: Final dough. Also, because the measurements for this recipe are precise, use a kitchen scale to weigh and measure the ingredients. King Arthur Flour Company (www.kingarthurflour. com) is a great online source for the barley flour, bread enhancer, and organic barley malt syrup.*

For the Poolish: (Make the day before)
9.6 ounces water
⅛ teaspoon instant dry yeast
9.6 ounces bread flour

For the Final Dough:
1.6 ounces Crystal 45 barley (available at home brewing supply stores)
11 ounces AleSmith Wee Heavy, room temperature

1.3 ounces water, room temperature
1 pound bread flour
6.4 ounces whole-wheat flour
2 ounces barley flour
1 tablespoon cocoa
1½ tablespoons brown sugar
¾ tablespoon salt
4 teaspoons bread enhancer
1¼ teaspoons instant dry yeast
1.6 ounces organic barley malt syrup

continued >

PERFECT PAIRING

WEE HEAVY is a Scotch Ale — a rich, malty brew with caramel and butterscotch notes. What you pair with this bread depends a lot on what you put on it. It would be delicious with butter or fresh jam. Or, as Peter says, "The bread holds up well with all kinds of cheeses, especially strong ones."

As soon as you put this bread to your lips, you notice its incredible aroma — it smells like all the warm, yeasty maltiness you get hit with when you walk into a brewery! When you take a bite, your mouth fills with the perfect combination of dense, chewy, crusty, and moist textures. As you would expect from a bread made by a brewer, this loaf delivers the wonderful flavors you love in a great beer: caramel, malt, and yeast — except this is like a beer you can chew!

ALESMITH'S WEE HEAVY ARTISAN BREAD

continued from page 22

[PREPARATION]

1. Make the poolish: Put the water in a medium bowl. Stir the yeast into the water, add the flour, and mix until smooth. Loosely cover with plastic wrap and let stand for 15 hours at 70°F.

2. Preheat oven to 350°F.

3. Make the final dough: Place the crystal barley on a clean baking sheet and bake for 2½ minutes. Shake the baking sheet and continue to bake for another 2½ minutes. Remove from the oven, let cool, then grind to a fairly fine texture (but not as fine as flour).

4. Bring the beer and water to room temperature. You want the final temperature of the dough to be about 75°F (use an instant-read thermometer).

5. Place all ingredients into a large mixing bowl, including the ground barley and the poolish.

6. Knead by hand in the bowl for 5 minutes. The consistency of the dough should be moderately loose. Add more water or flour to achieve the proper consistency.

7. Loosely cover the dough with plastic wrap and let ferment for 2 hours, folding the dough over once after the 1-hour mark.

8. Shape the dough into a single large, round loaf and place on a floured surface. Let rest for 15 minutes, then shape into a tight round loaf and return to the floured surface for 1½ hours at 75°F to rise.

9. Preheat a brick or Kamado-style oven, barbecue, or kitchen oven as well as a baking stone to 500°F.

10. Score the loaf as desired, cutting thinly along the surface as quickly as possible.

11. Fill a squeeze-trigger spray bottle with water and adjust to the finest setting. Spray three quick shots from the bottle into the oven just before you put the loaf in.

12. Use a pizza peel (lightly dusted with flour or cornmeal) to gently move the loaf from the floured surface to the baking stone, taking care not to deflate the loaf.

13. Monitor the baking carefully, especially after the 30-minute mark. The loaf can take up to 1 hour or longer to fully bake. When it is done, it will be light brown and sound like a drum when tapped.

ROASTED APPLE SOUP WITH HOPPY "GRILLED CHEESE"

KYLE BERGMAN, CHEF, GRILL AT THE LODGE AT TORREY PINES   *[serves 8]*

Chef's Note: *Making the hop extract takes at least 2 days.*

For the hop extract:
1 bottle Everclear grain
   alcohol
1 ounce fresh hops (I like
   Cascade or Amarillo.
   Available at home brew
   supply stores)

For the soup:
16 gala apples, peeled and
   cut in large dice
3 tablespoons butter, divided
   use

2 medium yellow onions, cut
   in large dice
2 large sprigs fresh rosemary
2 garlic cloves
2 cups apple cider
4 cups veal stock or broth
Salt and pepper, to taste
3 ribs celery, cut in small dice
2 persimmons, cut in small
   dice

For the cheese:
3 cups crumbled *queso fresco*

[PREPARATION]
1. Make the hop extract: In a bowl, soak the hops in the grain
alcohol for at least 48 hours, or longer, if possible.
2. Preheat oven to 400°F.
3. Make the soup: Place the apples on a baking sheet and roast
in the oven for 20 minutes.
4. In a large sauté pan over medium heat, melt 2 tablespoons

continued >

For pairing, Chef Kyle says, "I would have
something that complements the hop extract in
the grilled cheese — something like a pale ale or
an IPA — try to pick something that has a similar
hop profile to the hop you use in the oil."

**PERFECT
PAIRING**

*Kyle Bergman is one of San Diego's best-
known restaurant-based beer chefs. For
years, Kyle has done special beer dinners
at the Grill at the Lodge at Torrey Pines,
and he has participated in the food-centric
finales of San Diego Beer Week, which is
hosted by the Lodge each year.*

This simple dish is one of Kyle's favorite fall soups. "It has a really great balance between the sweetness of the apple and the spices, and the persimmon and celery add a beautiful crunch to the soup, which would be just a smooth purée without them." Kyle explains that the "grilled cheese" element was inspired by one of his line cooks from Tijuana, where chefs commonly grill queso fresco and add all sorts of ingredients to it "before it turns a toasty golden brown and they fold it over like a taco."

ROASTED APPLE SOUP WITH HOPPY "GRILLED CHEESE"

continued from page 25

of butter. Add the onions, rosemary, and garlic, and cook until the onion is softened but not browned. Add the apples, cider, and broth, and simmer for 20 minutes or so, until everything is soft.

5. Blend the mixture with an immersion blender or a counter-top blender and pass through a fine strainer. Season to taste with salt and pepper.

6. In a medium sauté pan over medium heat, melt 1 tablespoon of butter. Add the celery and cook until soft but not browned. Set aside.

7. Make the cheese: Heat a well-seasoned cast-iron skillet or nonstick pan. Sprinkle a small amount of the cheese in an even layer in the pan. Watch carefully: when the cheese starts to melt and brown, add 1 or 2 drops of hop extract — it will give off a great aroma!

8. Fold the melted and browned cheese over on itself like a taco and remove from pan. Heat soup to a boil. Ladle into bowls and garnish with persimmon and celery. Serve with the "grilled cheese" on the side.

THE CHICKS FOR BEER CHICA FRESCA SHRIMP CEVICHE

INGRID QUA, OWNER, HIGH DIVE BAR

[serves 10]

Chef's Note: *This recipe is best made the night before.*

2 large habanero peppers, diced*
12 ounces Ballast Point Sculpin IPA
1 medium purple onion, diced
2 medium yellow onions, diced
3 avocados, diced (not overly ripe)
1 large mango, diced
6 tomatoes, diced
6 small scallions, finely sliced
5 garlic cloves, finely chopped
1 bunch cilantro, finely chopped

2 pounds 30-50 count shrimp, cooked, peeled, deveined, and chopped
6 limes, juiced
1 tablespoon Sriracha Thai chile sauce
2 large jalapeño peppers, seeded and finely chopped*
1½ tablespoons salt
2 tablespoons freshly ground black pepper

[PREPARATION]

1. In a small bowl, combine the habaneros and the Sculpin. Let it sit for 1 hour.
2. In a large bowl, combine all the other ingredients and cover in plastic wrap until the habanero-infused Sculpin is ready.
3. Depending how much heat you want, you can either strain the habanero seeds out of the Sculpin before pouring it into the mix or keep them all in.
4. Add the Sculpin to the other ingredients, mixing gently to prevent ingredients from getting mushy. Cover in plastic wrap and let stand for a minimum of 1 hour. For best results, refrigerate overnight.

Note: Wear gloves when dicing peppers, and avoid touching your eyes.

Ingrid Qua started Chicks For Beer to provide a fun and appealing environment for women to learn about and appreciate beer. One thing she learned was that women love IPAs! And not wimpy IPAs — they love Sculpin and other serious beers. When Ingrid created this ceviche, it was a huge hit. "The Sculpin is so citrusy, it marries with the shrimp really well. And it marinates it well, too."

Ingrid loves to pair this dish with **BALLAST POINT'S HABANERO SCULPIN** or a similar pepper-infused IPA. Habanero Sculpin is a specialty beer that's mostly available in kegs, but you can always make your own (as you do for this recipe). If you want to counteract the heat in the ceviche, a pale ale or light Belgian ale would be a great choice.

PERFECT PAIRING

CLASSIC SAN DIEGO FISH TACOS
WITH CHIPOTLE LIME COLE SLAW

KAREN BERNAUER, GENERAL MANAGER, SAN DIEGO BREWING CO.   *[serves 4 or 2 as an entrée]*

"What's more Southern California than beer and fish tacos?" asks Karen Bernauer, chef and general manager at San Diego Brewing Co. "Everyone loves fish tacos and makes them in some form or another." Karen explains that this recipe is a particular customer favorite. "We use it frequently as a special, and it features our beer." At the brewery restaurant, they add a twist by using Chipotle Lime Cole Slaw instead of just plain cabbage.

For the cole slaw:
½ cup mayonnaise
½ cup sour cream
2 limes, zested and juiced
1 to 2 tablespoons canned
   chipotle peppers in adobo
½ teaspoon granulated sugar,
   optional
2 tablespoons white vinegar
Kosher salt and freshly ground
   black pepper, to taste
½ head green cabbage, shredded
½ cup red cabbage, shredded
¼ red onion, thinly sliced
3 green onions, thinly sliced
½ red bell pepper, thinly sliced
¼ cup fresh cilantro leaves,
   chopped

For the batter:
1 cup all-purpose flour
2 tablespoons cornstarch
½ teaspoon cumin
½ teaspoon salt
Freshly ground black pepper,
   to taste
1 egg
1 cup pale beer (I like Grantville
   Gold)
2 to 4 cups canola oil or vegetable
   oil, for frying fish, plus more for
   frying tortillas
1 pound cod filets, cut in 2- to
   3-ounce portions (or any mild
   white fish)
1 cup all-purpose flour, for dusting
   fish
1 package corn tortillas

continued >

PERFECT PAIRING

The spiciness of the cole slaw and crispy spiciness of the deep-fried fish make this a natural for a clean, light, hoppy ale. "We love to feature this with our **BALBOA EXTRA PALE ALE**," Karen says, but she adds that any great pilsner, Kolsch, or pale ale will work beautifully.

[PREPARATION]

1. Make the cole slaw: In a large bowl, whisk together mayonnaise, sour cream, lime zest and juice, chipotle peppers (start with 1 tablespoon, taste, and then add more if necessary), sugar, vinegar, and kosher salt and cracked black pepper to taste. Fold in the cabbage, onion, bell pepper, and cilantro. Refrigerate for at least 1 hour before serving.

2. Make the batter: In a large bowl, combine the flour, cornstarch, cumin, salt, and pepper. In a small bowl, whisk together the egg and beer, then stir into flour mixture. Set aside.

3. Preheat oil in a deep fryer to 375°F. Alternatively, in a heavy cast-iron skillet, heat approximately 2 cups of oil to near smoking. (Use enough oil to immerse the fish pieces.)

4. Cook the fish: Dust the fish filets lightly in flour, dip into the beer batter, and fry in the oil until crisp and golden brown.

5. In a skillet, heat 1 tablespoon of oil. Lightly fry the tortillas, one at a time, until they are heated but not too crisp. Drain on paper towels.

6. To assemble tacos, place a piece or two of fried fish in a tortilla and top with cole slaw.

Jason Danderand: "I especially love the notes of ginger, grains of paradise, and orange peel that Red Barn Ale adds to the soup. It's a beautiful, subtle beer that doesn't overpower the rest of the ingredients."

CAULIFLOWER, BEER, AND GRUYERE SOUP

JASON DANDERAND, BREWERY STAFF, PORT BREWING AND THE LOST ABBEY   *[serves 2]*

Chef's Note: *This recipe can be easily doubled or tripled.*

2 teaspoons butter
1½ cups onion, chopped
1½ cups celery, chopped
1½ tablespoons garlic, minced
2 to 3 pounds cauliflower, cut into
    small pieces
22 ounces saison-style beer
    (preferably Lost Abbey's Red Barn)

2 cups chicken or vegetable stock
1 cup whipping cream
2 cups Gruyere cheese, grated
    (divided use)
Cayenne pepper, to taste
Salt and pepper, to taste
½ baguette, sliced
Butter, for baguettes

[PREPARATION]

1. In a large stockpot over medium heat, melt the butter. Add the onions, celery, garlic, and cauliflower. Sauté until the onions are translucent and the cauliflower is tender.

2. Add the beer and stock, bring to a boil, and reduce heat. Cover and simmer for 15 to 20 minutes.

3. Add the cream and simmer for 15 minutes. Remove from heat and cool slightly.

4. Purée the soup with an immersion blender or a counter-top blender until smooth. Bring the soup back to a simmer and whisk in 1½ cups of cheese. Add the cayenne pepper, salt and pepper, and, if desired, more garlic, to taste.

5. Preheat oven to broil: Arrange baguette slices on a baking sheet, butter lightly, sprinkle with remaining cheese, and broil until golden brown and bubbling. Ladle soup into bowls and float cheesy toast on top.

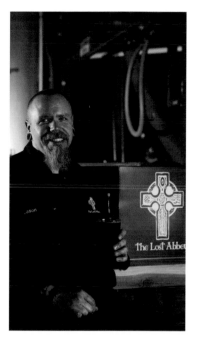

This recipe is a perfect example of what happens when a talented home cook takes the basic ideas from a recipe he likes and makes it his own. "The original recipe didn't have beer in it," explains Jason Danderand, "and it didn't have enough cream for my tastes, either."

LOST ABBEY'S RED BARN ALE is inspired by the traditional saison, or farmhouse ale. Its medium body and light, clean flavors work well with the subtle flavors of the cauliflower and other vegetables. You could also pair this with a bier de garde.

PERFECT PAIRING

CRAB-STUFFED WONTONS
IN MANZANITA BLONDE CREAMY TOMATO SAUCE

JESSE TRACY, BREWERY STAFF, MANZANITA BREWING CO.

[serves 4]

Jesse Tracy (center, pictured with Manzanita co-founders Garry Pitman, left, and Jeff Trevaskis) was inspired to create a recipe to highlight one of his favorite Manzanita beers, Riverwalk Blonde. "When I first tasted the blonde, I loved the combination of wheatiness and dryness — it has almost a Hefeweizen character to it," Jesse says. Originally, he tried a wonton filled with chicken, but "the meat didn't have the sweetness I was looking for to offset the hops in the beer." Then he tried crabmeat, and knew he had the right ingredients.

For the sauce:
2 tablespoons olive oil
5 cloves garlic, chopped
½ onion, chopped
1 (15-ounce) can diced stewed
 tomatoes
1 tablespoon fresh parsley,
 chopped
1 tablespoon fresh basil, chopped
1 tablespoon fresh oregano,
 chopped
¼ teaspoon salt
¼ teaspoon crushed red pepper
 flakes
½ tablespoon granulated sugar
⅛ teaspoon paprika
⅛ teaspoon freshly ground black
 pepper
¼ cup carrots, minced

1½ cups half-and-half
¾ cup Manzanita Blonde Ale

For the wontons:
16 ounces crabmeat (or imitation
 crabmeat)
½ cup Manzanita Blonde Ale
1 cup Italian cheese (I like Asiago,
 Romano, or Parmesan)
½ cup potato flakes
Dash of salt and pepper
1 squeeze lemon
1 package wonton wrappers
1 egg white
¼ to ½ cup olive oil, for frying

Finishing touches:
½ lemon
Chopped chives

continued >

PERFECT PAIRING

MANZANITA'S BLONDE is a Kolsch-style ale with light hoppiness and a clean, crisp character that pairs well with more subtle flavors. Other great Kolsch-style choices would be **IRON FIST'S RENEGADE BLONDE** or **MISSION BLONDE**.

[PREPARATION]

1. Make the sauce: In a medium saucepan over medium heat, heat the olive oil and sauté the garlic and onion until golden brown. Stir in the canned tomatoes, parsley, basil, oregano, salt, crushed red pepper, sugar, paprika, pepper, and carrots. Stir and simmer for 15 minutes. Add the beer and half-and-half. Remove from heat and purée with an immersion blender (or in a blender) to desired thickness. Return sauce to heat and simmer for 5 minutes.

2. Make the wontons: In large mixing bowl, combine crabmeat, beer, cheese, potato, salt, pepper, and lemon. Mix thoroughly. Place a tablespoon of the mixture in the center of each wonton square. Wet the edges of each wonton square with egg white, fold diagonally, and pinch the edges (pressing down with a fork works well). Heat the olive oil In a skillet and fry the wontons until golden brown on both sides.

3. To serve: Arrange wontons on a plate and squeeze a bit of lemon on them. Top wontons with sauce, or serve sauce on the side as a dipping sauce. Garnish with chives.

STONE'S TILAPIA CEVICHE

ALEX CARBALLO, CHIEF CULINARY PHILOSOPHER,
STONE BREWING WORLD BISTRO & GARDENS

[serves 6]

1 pound tilapia (or other sustainable fish)
1¼ cups fresh lemon juice
3 large tomatoes, cored, seeded, and diced
½ large cucumber, seeded and diced
½ jalapeño pepper, minced*
¼ cup cilantro, chopped, plus more for garnish
¼ cup red onion, diced
1 teaspoon all-natural ketchup (no corn syrup!)
1 teaspoon Tabasco sauce or Tapatio sauce
½ teaspoon Worcestershire sauce
Kosher salt and ground white pepper
Tortilla chips, for serving

[PREPARATION]

1. Cut the tilapia into ¼-inch cubes and put it in a large bowl. Add the fresh lemon juice, mix well, and let sit, refrigerated, for 2 hours.
2. Drain the excess juice from the tilapia and mix in the tomato, cucumber, jalapeño, cilantro, red onion, ketchup, Tabasco, and Worcestershire. Season with salt and white pepper to taste. Garnish with additional cilantro, if desired.
3. Serve immediately with tortilla chips, or store, covered and refrigerated, for up to 2 days.
Note: Wear gloves when mincing pepper, and avoid touching your eyes.

Chef Alex Carballo, from Stone Brewing World Bistro & Gardens, knows about fresh fish and especially about making great ceviche. He grew up in Mazatlan, Mexico, which is one of the world's game-fishing capitals. In Mazatlan, "ceviche is really big," Alex explains. "This is my family's recipe, to which I've added some personal touches. The Worcestershire and the ketchup are my additions. And I like a little spice, too, just to knock it up an inch." Alex says you can make this recipe with a wide variety of fish, including marlin, swordfish, shrimp, or the traditional Mexican white fish called sierra.

Alex says this dish is "perfect with an IPA because of the spice and the cilantro. The beer adds that really, really bright flavor to it. You could even go as far as a double IPA, like **STONE RUINATION IPA**. It pops it right out and makes you want to keep eating more because the hops complement the spice and cilantro so well."

PERFECT PAIRING

BEER CHEESE SOUP
WITH BLACK FOREST BACON AND PARMESAN GARLIC CROUTONS

DEREK FREESE, BREWMASTER, MONKEY PAW BREWERY

[serves 4]

"Beer cheese soup is kind of a classic dish for beer geeks around the world," explains Derek Freese, brewmaster and self-proclaimed "Head Ape" at Monkey Paw Brewery. "I've had a lot of beer cheese soups in my time, but I was never happy with most of them," he adds. "Most of them lacked depth, and a lot of times they're grainy and they use the wrong kind of beer. I wanted to create a recipe that combined a lot of flavors together in a harmonious way."

For the croutons:
1 loaf French bread, cut into cubes (slightly stale is good)
6 tablespoons butter, melted
3 cloves garlic, smashed
1 tablespoon fresh rosemary, finely chopped
½ cup Parmesan cheese, grated
Salt and pepper, to taste

For the soup:
¾ pound Black Forest bacon (or similar bacon), thick-cut, chopped into ½-inch pieces, plus 2 slices bacon for garnish
4 tablespoons butter

1 cup yellow onion, diced
3 cloves garlic, chopped
1 cup green onion, chopped
1 cup all-purpose flour
2 cups chicken stock, cold
2 cups half-and-half
½ pound aged sharp cheddar cheese, grated
½ pound aged Gruyere cheese, grated
2 teaspoons celery salt
1 habanero or other hot pepper, seeded and diced*
1 cup Pineapple X-Press (or similar beer, such as Ballast Point Pale Ale) at room temperature

[PREPARATION]
1. Make the croutons: Preheat oven to 375°F. (The croutons also can be toasted in a cast-iron skillet on the stove.)
2. In a bowl, toss the bread in the melted butter.

continued >

PERFECT PAIRING

At Monkey Paw, Derek brews a great extra-pale ale, **PINEAPPLE X-PRESS**, which has the crisp, bright hoppiness needed to counter a rich, fatty, cheesy soup. According to Derek, any great pale ale would do, and even a bright, citrusy IPA would work. "Sculpin would be great with this!"

Derek Freese: "I've made this recipe dozens of times and the most important step is using the highest-quality ingredients you can find."

Add the garlic and rosemary, and toss a little more. Mix in the grated Parmesan, and add salt and pepper to taste.

3. Bake for 7 to 10 minutes, or until browned. (The croutons should be a little soft but still golden brown.)

4. Make the soup: In a medium pan, cook the 2 pieces of bacon just until crisp. Break in half and set aside.

5. In a large soup pot, cook the remaining bacon over low heat until the fat is rendered but the bacon is not brown. Add the butter and melt it.

6. Add the yellow onion, garlic, and green onion and cook, stirring, until the onion is soft.

7. Add flour and whisk until it is incorporated into the butter. Add more butter if needed. The consistency should be grainy.

8. Cook the flour mixture for about a minute. It can bubble, but don't let it brown.

9. Slowly add the chicken stock and then the half-and-half. Stir constantly until incorporated.

10. Add the cheese slowly, stirring with a spatula or whisk.

11. Add the celery salt and habanero, and then stir in the beer. Start with 1 cup, adding more to taste.

12. Top with croutons and reserved bacon, and serve immediately.

Note: Wear gloves when dicing the peppers and avoid touching your eyes.

WASABI COLE SLAW

IRENE KOCH, STONE BREWING CO. MOM

[serves 8–10 as a side dish]

This slaw is delicious on its own, and it also makes a great accompaniment to a wide variety of things, including fish tacos and all kinds of burgers or sliders. "I try to keep my recipes simple," says Irene Koch, mother of Stone CEO & co-founder Greg Koch. "And Greg is always asking me to do more things vegan, so I often substitute mayonnaise with Veganaise." Try this slaw with recipes in this book.

For the slaw:
1 small head cabbage, chopped or shredded
4 green onions, thinly sliced
½ cup granulated sugar (or Splenda)
1 lemon, juiced

For the dressing:
½ cup grapeseed Veganaise (or mayonnaise)
½ cup Greek yogurt
1 teaspoon wasabi paste (or more, according to taste)

Finishing touches:
Poppy seeds
Garlic, minced
Fennel seeds
Fresh red bell peppers, chopped

[PREPARATION]
1. Make the slaw: In a large bowl, combine the cabbage and the green onions. Mix together.
2. Add the sugar (or Splenda) and sprinkle with the lemon juice. Mix together thoroughly.
3. Refrigerate for several hours to allow the flavors to combine.
4. Make the dressing: In a small bowl, combine all the dressing ingredients well and refrigerate until ready to serve.
5. To serve, combine the slaw with the dressing and mix well. If desired, sprinkle the slaw with poppy seeds, a small amount of garlic, and/or fennel seeds. Chopped red bell peppers can be added for color.

SPICY-O-LIFE BBQ BASTING OR DIPPING SAUCE

MIKE CAMPBELL, OPERATIONS MANAGER, IRON FIST BREWING CO. *[makes about 2 cups]*

Mike Campbell of Iron Fist Brewing explains that he and Brewmaster Brandon Sieminski "both love to cook with beer and both have food backgrounds, so we spend a lot of time pairing Iron Fist beers with food and coming up with new ways to use our brews in recipes." Mike adds that this BBQ sauce is very versatile, but it's particularly great with chicken, pork, or vegetables.

3 tablespoons vegetable oil
10 garlic cloves, smashed
½ to 1 whole habanero pepper
¼ cup pickled jalapeño pepper
1 (16-ounce) jar seedless
  raspberry jelly
½ cup honey
½ cup yellow mustard

¼ cup Dijon mustard
½ cup apple cider vinegar
1 teaspoon chipotle chile
  powder
750 milliliters (1 bottle) Iron
  Fist Spice of Life (or any great
  Belgian-style spiced ale)

[PREPARATION]

1. In a large pot on medium heat, combine the oil, garlic, habanero, and jalapeño, and cook until browned but not dark, about 2 minutes.

2. Add the jelly and honey, and stir until dissolved.

3. Add the mustards, vinegar, and chile powder. Stir together to combine, about 5 minutes.

4. Add the beer and bring to a boil. Reduce the heat and simmer until thick, about 30 minutes.

5. Strain to remove garlic and peppers. Use as a basting sauce for the last 5 minutes of cooking chicken, pork, beef, or vegetables, or use as a dipping sauce.

LONG BEANS TOPPED WITH A FRIED EGG

NEVA PARKER, HEAD OF LABORATORY OPERATIONS, WHITE LABS   *[serves 4]*

2 tablespoons soy sauce
1 tablespoon seasoned rice wine
   vinegar
1 teaspoon sesame oil
½ teaspoon chili oil
2 pounds Chinese long beans or
   green beans, sliced into 2- to
   3-inch pieces
1 teaspoon vegetable oil

2 cloves garlic, minced
3 dried Thai peppers or other
   spicy peppers, sliced thinly
1 (1-inch piece) ginger, peeled
   and minced
Canola or vegetable oil, for frying
4 large eggs
Salt and freshly ground black
   pepper, to taste

[PREPARATION]

1. Combine the first 4 ingredients in a small bowl and set aside.

2. Blanch beans in a pot of boiling salted water for 4 minutes, or until crisp-tender. Remove beans from water with a strainer and submerge in a bowl of ice water to stop the cooking.

3. Heat vegetable oil in a large wok or heavy frying pan on high heat. Be careful not to let the oil smoke. Add the garlic, Thai peppers, and ginger, stirring frequently until lightly browned and fragrant. Add the long beans and quickly stir-fry. Then add the sauce mixture and cook for another minute. Remove from heat.

4. Fry the eggs in a lightly-oiled pan until the whites are set but the yolks are still runny. Divide the beans among four plates, and top each plate with a fried egg. Finish with a sprinkling of salt and pepper.

"This is a recipe I've done a lot at home because it's really simple," says Neva Parker, head of Laboratory Operations at White Labs. "It just has a handful of ingredients, and it's really tasty," Neva says you can easily adjust the spice according to your taste, using more or fewer of the Thai peppers. Be sure to blanch the beans before you stir-fry them. You can also try topping the finished beans with different ingredients. "I added an egg because I just love fried eggs," Neva says.

The spiciness of this dish makes it a perfect companion for a hoppy, citrusy IPA, such as **GREEN FLASH'S WEST COAST IPA** or **ALPINE'S PURE HOPPINESS**. For a daring contrast, serve this with a smoky rausch beer or even a witbier, hefeweizen, or dunkelweizen with notes of cloves, spice, and citrus.

PERFECT PAIRING

BURGERS AND DOGS SURF & TURF
CHORIZO TURKEY SLIDER, ROASTED PEPPER CHILI, SPICY PICKLE CHIP AND SMOKED GOUDA BISCUIT WITH SHRIMP SAUSAGE AND CRAWFISH ÉTOUFFÉE

BRANDON HERNÁNDEZ, AWARD-WINNING FOOD-AND-BEER JOURNALIST   *[serves 4]*

San Diego food writer Brandon Hernández says he invented this dish as a "double amuse-bouche*" for his beer-centric supper club, Stein Diego. "It's a refined, beer-infused take on two American classics — chili dogs and chili cheeseburgers," he explains. "Instead of a chili dog, there's a shrimp-and-herb sausage. For the burger, I use turkey and augment it with pork chorizo."*

For the chili:
2 poblano chiles
2 Anaheim chiles
2 white chiles
4 red jalapeño peppers*
¼ cup vegetable oil
1 tablespoon olive oil
1 cup white onion, finely chopped
½ tablespoon cumin
1 teaspoon chili powder
½ teaspoon sweet paprika
½ teaspoon ground oregano
Salt, to taste
1 cup cooked black beans
½ tablespoon crushed garlic
1 bay leaf
¼ cup tomato paste
1½ cups beef stock
¾ cup red ale (I like Karl Strauss Red Trolley)

For the shrimp sausage:
1 pound medium shrimp, peeled and deveined
2 large egg whites
¼ cup parsley, chopped
2 teaspoons garlic, crushed
1 teaspoon vinegar-based hot sauce
¼ cup plus 1 tablespoon scallions, green parts only, sliced ¼-inch thick on the bias
Salt, to taste
¼ teaspoon white pepper

For the pickle chips:
[Makes about 30 chips]
2 medium cucumbers, sliced ¼-inch thick on the bias
¼ cup plus 2 tablespoons white vinegar   **continued >**

PERFECT PAIRING

The thickness and spice of the chili and étouffée yearn for a crisp, hop-forward beer to slice through them, providing a palate reboot. Brandon's perfect match for this dish is **THE PUPIL IPA** from Societe Brewing Co. It packs all the assertiveness of a West Coast IPA without the teeming bitterness, and it's downright juicy in its fruity profile.

Brandon Hernandez. "I love the way turkey takes on complementary flavors. It's the perfect canvas for veggie chili, roasted peppers, and some hand-crafted San Diego beer."

BURGERS AND DOGS SURF & TURF

continued from page 44

¼ cup granulated sugar
2 teaspoons salt
½ habanero chile*
½ teaspoon dill seed
½ teaspoon mustard seed
⅛ teaspoon celery seed

For the biscuits:

[Makes 16 biscuits]

1 cup all-purpose flour
½ tablespoon baking powder
¼ cup smoked Gouda cheese, finely grated
½ teaspoon salt
¼ teaspoon white pepper
¼ cup unsalted butter, cut into ½-inch cubes
¼ cup plus 2 tablespoons cold half-and-half
2 tablespoons unsalted butter, melted

For the étouffée:

6 tablespoons unsalted butter
1 cup yellow onion, finely chopped
¼ cup green bell pepper, finely chopped
¼ cup red bell pepper, finely chopped
½ cup celery, finely chopped
Salt and freshly ground black pepper, to taste
½ teaspoon garlic, minced
½ pound cooked crawfish tail meat, chopped
2 teaspoons Creole Spice Blend (see recipe page 84)
½ tablespoon Wondra flour
½ cup shrimp stock (or chicken stock)
1½ tablespoons parsley, finely chopped

For the turkey sliders:

1 pound ground turkey

5 ounces pork chorizo, casings removed
½ teaspoon dried ground oregano
2 teaspoons Dijon mustard
¾ teaspoon cumin
½ teaspoon Worcestershire sauce
Salt, to taste
2 tablespoons olive oil

[PREPARATION]

1. Preheat oven to 325°F.

2. Start the chili: Coat the chiles and jalapeño with the vegetable oil and place on a baking sheet lined with aluminum foil. Place in the oven and roast until the chiles are soft and the skins are blackened in spots, about 1 hour.

3. Make the sausage: Combine the shrimp, egg whites, parsley, garlic, hot sauce, ¼ cup of the scallions, 1 teaspoon of salt, and white pepper in a food processor and pulse until blended. Transfer one-quarter of the mixture to a sheet of plastic wrap. Form into an even strip and roll into a log. Wrap tightly, tying knots at each end, and refrigerate for at least 1 hour.

4. Make the pickles: Place the cucumbers in a shallow microwaveable dish. Whisk the vinegar and sugar together. Add the remaining ingredients and pour the mixture over the cucumbers. Place the dish in the microwave and heat on high for 3 minutes. Let cool to room temperature. Strain the cucumbers and serve, or place with liquid in an airtight container.

5. Remove the chiles from the oven and transfer to a bowl. Cover with plastic wrap and let steam for 20 minutes.

6. Raise oven temperature to 350°F.

7. Uncover and remove the skin from the chiles, stemming and seeding them in the process. Chop and set aside.

8. Make the biscuits: Combine the flour, baking powder,

Brandon says, "I've always adored Creole cooking, and I love to use traditional Creole spices in a lot of my beer-friendly recipes."

cheese, salt, and pepper in a mixing bowl. Cut in the butter until it is fully incorporated. Gently fold in the half-and-half until the dough forms a ball. Turn the dough out onto a lightly floured surface, sprinkle with additional flour, and fold the dough into itself until it is no longer sticky. Gently press the dough into a 1-inch thick square. Use a 2-inch ring mold to cut out 4 round biscuits and place them on a greased baking sheet. Use a 2-inch by 1-inch rectangular mold to cut out 4 rectangular biscuits and place them on the sheet. Brush the tops of the biscuits with butter and bake until golden brown, 12 to 15 minutes. Remove from the oven and slice in half lengthwise. Set aside.

9. Finish the chili: Heat the olive oil in a large pot or Dutch oven over medium-high heat. Add the onion, and season with cumin, chili powder, paprika, oregano, and salt. Cook until soft and tender, 5 to 6 minutes. Add the beans, garlic, and bay leaf, and cook, stirring, for 1 minute. Add the tomato paste and roasted chiles, stirring, for 1 minute. Stir in the stock and beer, and bring to a boil. Reduce heat to medium-low and simmer until the chili thickens, about 40 minutes. Discard the bay leaf and use an immersion blender to slightly purée, leaving a bit of texture. Keep warm or refrigerate in an airtight container for up to 1 week.

10. Boil the sausage: Heat a gallon of water in a large pot over medium heat. Place the plastic-wrapped shrimp sausage in the pot, making sure to prevent it from bending, and cook until the shrimp mixture has solidified, about 10 minutes. Remove from the pot and let cool to room temperature.

11. Make the étouffée: Melt the butter in a large skillet over medium heat. Add the onion, bell peppers, and celery. Season with salt and pepper, and sauté until soft and tender, about 8 minutes. Add the garlic and cook, stirring, for 1 minute. Season the crawfish with the spice blend and add to the skillet, stirring occasionally, for 1 minute. Dissolve the flour in the stock and add to the skillet. Stir until the mixture thickens slightly. Reduce the heat to medium-low and simmer for 6 to 8 minutes, stirring occasionally. Add the parsley, reduce heat to low, and keep warm.

12. Make the sliders: In a large mixing bowl, combine the turkey, chorizo, oregano, mustard, cumin, and Worcestershire sauce. Season with salt to taste and form the mixture into 12 (2-inch) round patties. Heat the oil in a large skillet over medium heat. Place the patties in the skillet, 6 at a time, and sear until browned and cooked through, 3 to 4 minutes on each side. Transfer the patties to a plate lined with paper towels and dab off any excess oil. Set aside and keep warm. Add the shrimp sausages to the skillet and brown on all sides, about 30 seconds per side. Remove from the heat and keep warm.

13. To serve, place a round biscuit half on the left side of a rectangular plate. Top with a slider and nappé with chili. Place a pickle atop the slider and lean the other half of the biscuit against the slider. Cut the sausages into 3-inch segments. Place two rectangular biscuit halves side-by-side on the right side of the plate. Place a sausage segment on top of the biscuits and nappé with étouffée. Sprinkle the remaining scallions around the plate and serve immediately.

Note: Wear gloves when chopping peppers, and avoid touching your eyes.

Pairing Beer and Cheese: Ideas and Inspirations

Most people think of wine when they think of cheese tasting. (Who hasn't been to the classic informal social get-together known as the "wine & cheese"?) The truth is that beer can provide a much more interesting and varied experience than wine when tasting cheeses (or any kind of food). The vast variety of beers, with their almost infinite combination of aromas and flavors, can offer the adventurous gourmand a uniquely complex and very satisfying experience. And let's face it: beer is just fun!

There are so many cheeses in the world, and there are so many beers, how do you even start to plan a simple beer and cheese event? Well, there are no hard-and-fast rules — except that you should always go with things you like — or things you'd like to taste. Even though there are basic guidelines for what makes a good pairing, every guideline is subject to your own palate. Only you can decide if a pairing works for you. What tastes like grapefruit to one person may taste like cinnamon to another.

Mimolette from France, part of the first course pairing with Ballast Point Calico Amber Ale.

Mary Palmer (above, left) from Taste Cheese provided the cheese expertise at our event. Tom Nickel (above, center) and Tyson Blake (above, right) provided background and tasting notes on all the fabulous beers.

So, where to start? First, let's assume you're already somewhat familiar with beer styles and some of the different flavor profiles that each kind of beer can offer. (If not, flip to the front flap of this book and take a look at the Basic Beer Styles chart.) Second, make sure you've got a general overview of how the world of cheese is organized.

Every cheese has two basic character traits: its texture and its strength of flavor. There are generally four basic textures and four basic strengths. On the texture side, a cheese will either be soft, semi-soft, semi-hard, or hard. On the strength side, a cheese will either be mild, medium, bold, or strong. If you keep this rule of "4 and 4" in the back of your mind when putting together a tasting event, it will help you organize your thoughts and zero in on the kinds of beers you might want to pair.

For the purposes of pairing, it's probably best to focus on the four basic cheese strengths, as that will govern the flavors you'll want to complement or contrast with the beers you pair. The chart on the back flap of this book (The Four Quadrants of Cheese) is organized by the four categories of cheese strength, with suggestions for beers that traditionally pair best with each grouping. Again, use this as a guideline, but remember that the most exciting moments at

any tasting are those unexpected results you get from experimenting and improvising. That's where the magic really happens.

After you've considered the chart on the back flap, you can start thinking about putting together your own pairing event. As you do, read through the menu lineup that follows. This was an epic beer-and-cheese pairing at O'Brien's Pub with one of San Diego's premier cheese educators, Mary Palmer of Taste Cheese. That night, O'Brien's owner, Tom Nickel, and O'Brien's GM, Tyson Blake, broke out some truly special beers and paired them with some truly amazing cheeses.

We hope that the photos and descriptions that follow will inspire you to explore the exciting world of beer and cheese, and will lead you to many new and surprising taste discoveries!

FIRST COURSE
• **Mimolette (mild, semi-hard) paired with Ballast Point Calico Amber Ale**
• **Parmigiano-Reggiano (medium, hard) paired with Firestone Double Barrel Ale**

Tom Nickel began the night by introducing the basics of the first pairings: "Even though these cheeses are pretty different, the beers are actually quite

Fresh, crunchy Parmigiano-Reggiano paired perfectly with Firestone Double Barrel Ale.

similar. You might find that you like them with the cheese we paired on the menu, or you might like each better with the other cheese. That's the beauty of these tastings: it's all very subjective. If you think it tastes good, then it's a good pairing."

Tom explained the beers: "Ballast Point Calico is a classic amber with rich maltiness, been around a long time; it's a great beer and a San Diego fixture. Firestone Double Barrel is one of the coolest craft beers brewed in the industry. No matter how much

of this beer they make, 20 percent of it is always fermented in oak barrels. This gives the beer a really unique roundness that you won't find in any other English-style pale."

Then Mary Palmer took the floor and provided a little background on the cheeses: "The Mimolette, from France, is such a striking cheese, I always love to include it wherever I can. The color is fantastic — it looks like a cantaloupe — and the texture is very similar to a cheddar, with a wonderful lushness

Lindsey Nickel's warm, melty, fried Camembert was perfect with Green Flash's Rayon Vert, a Belgian-inspired pale ale.

to it. The amber ale has a richness that pairs with the cheese's texture, but it also has the hoppiness to refresh the palate after the yummy fat has coated your tongue."

"The other cheese, the Parmagiano, I love to use as a frame of reference," Mary continued. "Everybody's had parm before, but this one is really fresh, so it's not dried out, and you get that crunchy delicious grit in there — the enzymes starting to calcify. I love it with the malty richness of the DBA, which has just a little bit of hop. It's really one of the classic pairings that we've done."

SECOND COURSE:
• Fried Camembert (mild, soft) with Mango Chutney paired with Green Flash Rayon Vert Belgian Pale

Tom Nickel took us through the basics of the next course: "This pairing was one that Tyson insisted we do. It's my wife Lindsey's recipe and it's one of our all-time favorites." Tyson chimed in, "And we even used some of the Rayon Vert in the chutney to create this great combination of salty and sweet, which contrasts with that funky, delicious Camembert."

Tom went on to say, "This beer is relatively new to the Green Flash lineup. Green Flash owner Mike Hinkley said that, if Green Flash were in Belgium, this would be his West Coast IPA, his flagship beer." Tom explained that Rayon Vert (which means "Green Flash" in French) is a Belgian golden ale that is bottled with Brettanomyces (wild yeasts). "That's what they do with the famous Belgian beer Orval. It's not brewed with wild yeasts, but it's bottled with wild yeasts. And, although it takes a little while for the yeast character to fully develop — to get that real earthiness to the beer — you see after six months or so that really delicious funk that comes with Brett beers."

Mary offered some background on the Camembert that was paired with the Rayon Vert.

The sharp flavors of peppers stuffed with goat cheese were perfectly offset by the hoppiness of two great IPAs.

"People are always asking me what's my favorite cheese, and, honestly — if I had to choose — I'd say Camembert." Mary explained that this particular cheese comes from the best producer in France and is aged "by a guy whose sole job it is to age cheese." Mary described the many complex flavors in this cheese as "a mix of cauliflower, nuttiness, and funk that merges brilliantly with the beer."

THIRD COURSE
• Peppadew Peppers stuffed with Purple Haze Goat Cheese (bold, soft) paired with Alpine O'Brien's IPA and Julian Brewing Co. 1870 IPA.

Tom was a little sheepish about this pairing, because it featured two beers that he actually brewed. Luckily, Tyson had convinced him that this was must-have addition to the menu. Tom said, "For the Alpine collaboration, Pat McIlheney and I wanted to do something along the lines of a Blind Pig IPA or Avery IPA — nice and hoppy but not super strong." The other beer, the Julian Brewing IPA, was brewed by

Tom in Julian. "And again, I wanted an IPA that wasn't too over-the-top in terms of alcohol. It uses a new hop blend from Hop Union called Zythos, which I had wanted to try. It's got a real nice piney, citrus character with a nice sweetness that balances really well with the peppers."

For the cheese notes, Mary began, "One thing about IPAs is that the really sharp flavors of sharp cheeses go beautifully with really hoppy beers, and they start to bring out some of the secondary characteristics in both the beer and the cheese." The peppadew peppers traditionally come from only one place in the world — South Africa — and they are a special combination of sweet and heat. The Purple Haze goat cheese has lavender and fennel pollen in it. "In Central California, fennel grows wild all over the place," Mary said. "In its pollen form, it's really floral and aromatic, as is the lavender. When you combine the sharp flavors of the cheese, the heat and sweet of the peppers, and then you throw in the hoppiness of the IPAs, it's such a great combination of flavors."

Rich, nutty Gruyere paired wonderfully with Belgian heavy-hitter Malheur Dark Brut Brouwerj de Landtsheer.

FOURTH COURSE
• Gruyere (medium, hard) paired with Malheur Dark Brut Brouwerij de Landtsheer

Tom stood up and smiled. "It's not common, when we do these beer and cheese tastings, that in course four we're introducing a 12 percent beer," he began. "But this beer is just a great beer. It's got a lot of really food-friendly flavors, it's dark but not roasty, not too heavy, and it does not drink like a 12 percent beer. The combination of the Gruyere with the brut is, to me, one our most perfect pairings."

Mary added a few thoughts about the cheese: "Because you have a beer with this kind of heft, you need a cheese — an Alpine cheese, like this raw-milk Gruyere — that develops texture as it ages, until it gives you a rich, nutty, fudgy, fatty texture in your mouth that just pairs beautifully with the bubbles and the rich maltiness of this dark and yeasty brew."

FIFTH COURSE
• Montgomery Cheddar (medium, semi-hard) paired with North Coast Old Stock Ale

"Old Stock is kind of a throwback to the original English-style barleywine," Tom explained. "It was traditionally a strong beer that breweries kept around for special occasions. It's got massive dark fruit, strong sweet malt characteristics, and just a great richness to it. I love this beer." Tom also explained that Old Stock and similar barleywines can really evolve beautifully over time. "I've had Old Stock at 3, 4, 5 years and it was amazing."

Mary said a few words about the cheddar: "English-style cheddars like this one are bound in cheesecloth and then aged in a cave," Mary explained. "And the cheese is somewhat porous, so it soaks up all the earthy components of the cave. And sometimes there's a fissure in the cheese and there are all these spores floating around, and they get in the cheese.

This earthy, cavey, blue Montgomery Cheddar was wonderful with the North Coast Old Stock Ale, an English-style barleywine.

That creates the bluing, and the bluing adds such a complexity to the cheese — a real earthiness that I call the cavey deliciousness."

SIXTH COURSE
- **Boucheron (bold, soft) paired with Verhaughe Duchesse de Bourgogne and Young's Double Chocolate Stout**

"This is what we call the chocolate-cherry-cheesecake pairing," Tom began, by way of introduction. "The Boucheron is an amazing goat cheese. You get different textures from it, going inside to outside. You eat it and it really coats your mouth. You get that super-creamy flavor that gets into your cheeks, coats your tongue, your teeth, and then you take a sip of beer, and it washes it all away. That's one of things that I really love about pairing beer and cheese. The carbonation in beer acts as a cleanser in your mouth in a way that most wines will not. The carbonation brings the flavors up off your tongue and actually really helps to blend them. In that way, you really are pairing them."

Tom went on to say, "These two beers couldn't be more different. You have the sweet chocolate stout from Young's, and the Duchesse is a Flemish brown ale, barrel-aged, with sour cherry flavors. It's something that's 8 months old blended with older beer. These two beers are so different, and yet they both complement this cheese so well. To me it's really a great example of how varied beer can be and how well different components of very different beers can all work well together."

Mary was quick to chime in on this one. "I do get really excited by the alchemy of pairing, and this is a great example of that. So here's how it's done. Start with a sip of beer. The Duchesse. Coat your mouth with the flavors of beer. A little tart. Pomegranate, some people say. Then take a bite of the cheese and another sip of the Duchesse. Boom! Cherry cheesecake! Now drink down the Duchesse and add the stout to it. Take another bite of the cheese and then a sip of the mixed beers. Boom! Chocolate cherry cheesecake!"

SEVENTH COURSE
• **Stilton (strong, semi-hard) paired with AleSmith Old Numbskull Barleywine**

For the final course, Tom, Tyson, and Mary rolled out yet another perfect pairing that left everyone wanting more. As Tom explained, "This was something new that Tyson cooked up for us. It's a Stilton fondue with little zucchini bread bites and thick-cut bacon. It's got the sweetness, the saltiness, and the rich fatty texture that makes it a really satisfying ending to the evening." Tyson went on to explain, "AleSmith Old Numbskull is such a classic beer. It's nutty, malty, and got a wonderfully complex, wine-like character. Pairing barleywine with Stiltons and blues is a classic strategy, and when you taste them together you see why. We love this beer. It's very food friendly, and it's just a classic combination of flavors."

Boucheron tasted amazing when paired with Verhaughe Duchesse de Bourgogne and Young's Double Chocolate Stout (Chocolate Cherry Cheesecake!)

Tyson Blake's warm, creamy Stilton fondue was the perfect sweet-and-salty ending to the evening. Paired with AleSmith's Old Numbskull Barleywine, it was magic.

main courses

WAHOO WHEAT CIOPPINO

JUAN MIRON AND SARA FRIEDMAN, MIHO GASTROTRUCK   *[serves 4]*

MIHO Gastrotruck has become a fixture in the San Diego beer and brewery scene. Wherever it shows up, long lines begin to form. Sara Friedman, MIHO chef and recipe developer (above, with Juan Miron), created this dish for a special event at a San Diego brewery. "We wanted to break out of the typical foods that are usually cooked/paired with beers and try something different," Sara recalls.

For the broth:
1 to 2 tablespoons olive oil
2 large yellow onions, quartered
  with peels on
5 garlic cloves
1 stalk celery
2 carrots, cut into large chunks
  (unpeeled)
22 ounces Ballast Point Wahoo
  Wheat
2 cups chicken stock
6 Roma tomatoes, blanched,
  peeled, and chopped (or use a
  14-ounce can of peeled Roma
  tomatoes)
1 fennel top
1 pinch saffron (a small pinch!)

For the seafood:
1 to 2 tablespoons olive oil
1 medium yellow onion, cut in
  small dice
1 stalk celery, cut in small dice

2 carrots, cut in small dice
6 cloves garlic, minced
3 medium russet potatoes, cut
  in small dice and roasted
1 pound clams
1 pound mussels
1 pound (21/25) Mexican white
  shrimp, butterflied
Kosher salt, to taste
Freshly ground black pepper,
  to taste
Crushed red pepper, to taste,
  if desired
½ cup fresh parsley, chopped
¼ cup fresh dill, chopped
⅛ cup fennel tops, chopped
2 tablespoons fresh oregano,
  chopped
¼ cup butter, cold, cut into
  pieces

Finishing touch:
Crusty bread, toasted **continued >**

PERFECT PAIRING

The obvious choice is **WAHOO WHEAT** or other great wheat-style beers, such as **LIGHTNING'S THUNDERWEIZEN, NEW ENGLISH'S WHY? NOT**, or even some lighter Belgian-inspired brews, such as **IRON FIST'S HIRED HAND**. Says Sara: "**SCULPIN IPA** is also a great choice too, with its citrus notes."

Sara Friedman: "We created this recipe because we wanted to do something a little more interactive with our guests — and any excuse I can get to cook seafood, I take."

[PREPARATION]

1. Make the broth: In a large pot, heat the olive oil and sauté the onions, garlic, celery, and carrots until they are softened but not browned. Add beer and stock, and bring to a simmer. Add tomatoes and mix thoroughly. Add fennel and saffron and simmer for 15 minutes. Strain broth and set aside.

2. In a deep skillet or wok, heat olive oil and sauté onions, celery, carrots, garlic, and potatoes. Add clams and cook for about 1 minute. Add mussels and cook for about 1 minute more. Add shrimp and season with salt, pepper, and red pepper, if desired. Sauté for about 1 minute and add broth (just enough to come halfway up the pan). Taste and adjust seasoning if needed.

3. Add the parsley, dill, fennel, and oregano, and stir to mix. Then add cold butter. Discard any clams or mussels that fail to open. Once the clams and mussels are open and the butter has melted, you can start eating!!

JUDGMENT DAY STEAMED CARLSBAD MUSSELS
WITH ANDOUILLE SAUSAGE, EGGPLANT, AND MUSHROOMS

BERNARD GUILLAS, EXECUTIVE CHEF, THE MARINE ROOM

[serves 6]

1 tablespoon olive oil
1 cup Andouille sausage, sliced
1 cup eggplant, cut in small dice
¼ cup shallots, chopped
½ pound king trumpet mushrooms, sliced
1 medium leek, white part only, washed, patted dry, and diced
1 small fennel bulb, cored, cut into 8 wedges

4 pounds black mussels, scrubbed, beards removed
⅔ cup Lost Abbey Judgment Day (or other dark, rich Belgian-style quad)
¼ teaspoon cumin seeds
1 lemon, zested
Freshly ground black pepper, to taste
Pinch sea salt
¾ cup heavy cream
¼ cup flat-leaf parsley, chopped
Sourdough bread slices, grilled

[PREPARATION]

1. Heat olive oil in large stock pot over medium heat. Add Andouille sausage, eggplant, shallots, mushrooms, leeks, fennel, and cook without browning, stirring often for 3 minutes.

2. Add the mussels, beer, cumin seeds, lemon zest, black pepper and sea salt. Cover. Raise heat to high. Cook 3 minutes or until liquid starts to boil and steam comes out from under the lid.

3. Uncover and stir in cream. Using a slotted spoon, rotate mussels from bottom to top for even cooking. Cover, and cook until all shells open.

4. Transfer the mussels to large serving bowl. Pour the broth over mussels, and sprinkle with parsley. Serve with grilled sourdough bread.

"What I love most about **JUDGMENT DAY** is the intense flavor and earthiness of the beer," Bernard says. "That's what really makes this dish. The combination of the rich beer, the smokiness of the sausage, and the delicate briny flavors of the mussels is just beautiful." Other great quad beers: **KARL STRAUSS'S TWO TORTUGAS** or **IRON FIST'S DUBBEL FISTED**.

PERFECT PAIRING

"This is a great summer dish," explains Bernard Guillas, executive chef at La Jolla's Marine Room, one of San Diego's most highly praised and best-loved seafood restaurants. "It's simple, quick, and you can even do it outside on the barbecue." Bernard also loves to make this dish with local ingredients, including local mushrooms, local produce, and the famous and delicious Carlsbad mussels that are farmed only a few miles up the coast from the restaurant.

GREEN FLASH BARLEYWINE-GLAZED SALMON

CHUCK SILVA, BREWMASTER, GREEN FLASH BREWING CO.   [serves 8]

Brewmaster Chuck Silva has been serious about pairing beer and food for a long time, and this recipe is one of his favorites. "I first developed this for an event we did with Hamilton's Tavern," Chuck recalls. "We used a barleywine that had a few years of age on it, and it was great."

Chef's Notes: *Start this recipe 12 to 24 hours ahead. I prefer the mild flavors of cherrywood, but alder works well, and a blend of the two is very nice. Two hours is a good timeframe for smoking the salmon — more or less depending on the heat intensity of your charcoal. As the salmon smokes and cooks through, the juices will begin to come up to the surface and will form some protein globules. Simply brush the protein globules away as you coat the salmon with the glaze. Test the salmon fillets for doneness by gently pressing on a fillet. The surface should "break," and the center should be very tender but moist and flaky.*

3 cups brown sugar (divided use)
1 cup coarse sea salt
6 cups water
2 salmon (or steelhead) sides, filleted
22 ounces Green Flash Barleywine
4 large handfuls cherry and/or alder wood chips, soaked
    according to directions

[PREPARATION]

1. Brine the salmon: Combine 2 cups of the brown sugar and the coarse sea salt in 6 cups cold water to make brine for the salmon.

continued >

PERFECT PAIRING

Chuck says, "**GREEN FLASH BARLEYWINE**, which has a huge caramel maltiness, would be nice to try with the salmon, but having it with a full meal may be a bit too much. I would have something that's a little more refreshing and effervescent, something that cuts through the fattiness of the fish. You could even do a trippel. Our **TRIPPEL** is dynamite with this salmon."

2. Place the salmon in the brine in a non-reactive container. (You can use 2 large zipper-top bags, 1 for each fillet, dividing the brine in half.) Refrigerate the salmon in the brine for 12 to 24 hours, turning occasionally.

3. Preheat a grill or smoker to medium-low heat (200 to 225°F).

4. Smoke the salmon: Remove the salmon from its brine and pat dry with paper towels. Place the fillets on the grill or in a smoker (skin side down) for indirect cooking. Put a handful of water-soaked wood chips directly on the charcoal or grill stones to begin the smoking. Close the lid. If you are using a conventional charcoal grill, leave the vents closed or only slightly cracked. Smoke for about 2 hours.

5. Make a glaze: In a small saucepan on medium-low heat, melt the remaining cup of brown sugar in 11 ounces of the barleywine, stirring occasionally. (Pour the remaining 11 ounces of barleywine in your favorite snifter-type beer glass and sip while the salmon is smoking!) Simmer until the liquid is reduced by about one-third. (The beer foam will gradually subside.)

6. Brush the salmon with some of the glaze. Add another handful of soaked wood chips and charcoal to the fire, if needed. Rotate the grill if the coals are uneven and replace the lid for further smoking. Repeat the glazing two or three more times, adding wood chips and charcoal as needed.

SMALL BAR'S BEER-BATTER FISH WITH REMOULADE

BRIAN HICKS, KITCHEN MANAGER, SMALL BAR,
AND LOUIS MELLO, GENERAL MANAGER, SMALL BAR

[serves 4]

(Pictured above: Louis Mello, left; Brian Hicks, right) Karen Blair remembers when she and husband Scot were first planning to open Small Bar. "Scot was adamant," Karen recalls. "He wanted Small Bar to have the best fish and chips in town. So we set out and we tried many versions — many, many versions (Scot is a perfectionist!) — and finally we hit on this recipe. Now it's our top seller."

Chef's Note: *This dry batter mix makes enough for 2 batches. For each batch, add 3½ cups of beer to the dry mix (3½ cups). You may need to add a little more beer to get the batter to the right consistency — not too thick or too thin. Test a piece of fish to see how the batter clings.*

For the remoulade:
1 cup capers
1 splash caper brine
½ cup pepperoncini, sliced
½ cup fresh dill, chopped
½ bunch of fresh parsley
1 lemon, juiced
2 cups mayonnaise

For the batter:
(Makes 2 batches)
5 cups rice flour
1¼ cups cornstarch
⅓ cup onion powder
3 tablespoons garlic powder
2 tablespoons black pepper
⅓ cup salt
3 tablespoons smoked paprika

For each batch:
Mix dry ingredients with 3½ cups
   of Anchor Steam

For the fish:
3 pounds fresh white fish, cut into 12
   serving pieces (cod, haddock, or halibut
   works well)
1 cup all-purpose flour
1 cup cornstarch
Canola oil, for frying

Finishing Touches:
Chips (French fries)!
Fresh lemon wedges

continued >

PERFECT PAIRING

ANCHOR STEAM is a great pairing for this dish, but battered and fried foods will also work very well with lighter, crisper beers, such as pilsners (**LIGHTNING'S ELEMENTAL** is excellent), Kolsch-styles (**IRON FIST'S RENEGADE BLONDE**), extra pales (**ALESMITH'S X**), and Belgian pale ales.

[PREPARATION]

1. Make the remoulade: In a food processer, combine all the ingredients except the mayonnaise. Process until the mixture has the consistency of a thin pesto. Add the mayonnaise and process again until all ingredients are fully incorporated and mixture is light green in color. Chill until ready to serve.

2. Mix the dry ingredients for the batter: In a large bowl, combine all dry ingredients. For one recipe (3 pounds/12 pieces of fish), measure out half of the dry mix and add 3½ cups of beer.

3. Mix the flour and cornstarch together to make a dredge. Coat each piece of fish completely in the dredge.

4. Dip each piece of fish into the batter, making sure you cover completely.

5. Heat oil in a deep-fryer or heavy bottom stockpot to 350°F, or pour 1 inch of oil into a cast-iron skillet and heat until it is near smoking. Use tongs to place a few pieces of fish into the oil. (Keep a grip on the fish for 10 seconds so it doesn't stick to the bottom of the pot. If you don't to this, the fish will rip apart when you pull it out.) Fry fish until golden brown.

BROWN BUTTER-SEARED SCALLOPS
WITH IPA GASTRIQUE, HOP FLOWER DUST, AND CANDIED PEANUTS

KATHERINE HUMPHUS, EXECUTIVE CHEF, BO-BEAU KITCHEN + BAR   *[serves 4]*

Chef's Note: *Dried hop flowers are available at home brew stores.*

For the peanuts:
2 cups raw peanuts
1 cup granulated sugar
⅓ cup water

For the gastrique:
¼ cup granulated sugar
1 tablespoon champagne vinegar
1 cup freshly squeezed orange juice
1 cup Wipeout IPA

For the scallops:
2 teaspoons olive oil or canola oil
12 scallops (U-10 size)
Salt and freshly ground black pepper
3 tablespoons butter

Finishing touch:
1 dried hop flower, finely chopped, keep in an airtight container

[PREPARATION]
1. Make the peanuts: In a wide, heavy skillet, mix the peanuts with the sugar and water. Cook over moderate heat, stirring frequently, until the liquid seizes up. It will take a few minutes. The peanuts will get crusty and the sugar will crystallize. Then the peanuts will become dry and sandy. (Don't worry; you didn't mess up!)

continued >

"I love doing contrasting flavors," says Katherine Humphus, executive chef at the popular French bistro Bo-Beau, *"and I wanted to do something really different for this recipe."* She decided that beer and scallops don't usually go together, so scallops would be the centerpiece of this dish. Then she thought about combining sweet and savory elements, along with a bitter component. *"That's how we came up with the IPA gastrique along with candied peanuts,"* she says.

To pair with this dish, Katherine suggests something that's "not overpowering" because scallops have a delicate flavor. Even though she uses a boldly hopped IPA in the gastrique, she actually recommends drinking a more restrained IPA or pale ale with the dish. "Even a hefeweizen would go nicely," she adds.

PERFECT PAIRING

Katherine Humphus: *"Sweetness from the scallops and peanuts combined with the savory elements from the IPA — that's the centerpiece of this dish."*

BROWN BUTTER-SEARED SCALLOPS
continued from page 69

2. Lower the heat and keep going, scraping up any syrup on the bottom of the pan and stirring the peanuts into it, coating them as much as possible.

3. As you go, tilt the pan, removing it from the heat from time to time to regulate the heat so you can coat the nuts with the liquid as it darkens without burning the peanuts or the syrup. This is the only tricky part — I like to get the peanuts as deeply-bronzed as possible. If the mixture starts to smoke, remove it from the heat and stir.

4. When the peanuts are a deep bronze color, take them off the heat and transfer to a bowl to cool.

5. Make the gastrique: Heat the sugar in a heavy medium saucepan on medium heat until it begins to melt. Stir until all of the sugar dissolves. Then cook with minimal stirring.

6. Add the vinegar. The mixture will harden — do not be alarmed! Stir until caramel melts, about 1 minute.

7. Add the orange juice and the beer. Boil until the mixture is reduced by three-quarters to a generous ½ cup, about 15 minutes.

8. Prepare the scallops: Heat the oil in a sauté pan on medium-high heat.

9. Pat the scallops dry with a paper towel and season with salt and pepper. Once the pan is very hot and starts smoking slightly, add the scallops. Cook only 4 scallops at a time to avoid overcrowding the pan.

10. The scallops are ready to flip over once they begin to turn golden brown, about 1 to 2 minutes. Once you flip the scallops, add the butter. The scallops are done once sides are firm, after about 2 to 3 minutes.

11. Serve the scallops drizzled with the gastrique, a small amount of hop flower dust, and finely chopped candied peanuts.

STEAMED BLACK COD
WITH MAITAKE MUSHROOMS AND MANILA CLAMS IN ALESMITH HORNY DEVIL NAGE

SCHUYLER SCHULTZ, ALESMITH CULINARY DIRECTOR /
CHEF, THE VINE COTTAGE

[serves 4]

For the sauce:
2 garlic cloves, minced
1-inch piece fresh ginger,
  peeled, grated
1 to 2 Thai chiles, chopped*
  (depending on your spice
  preference)
2 limes, juiced
2 tablespoons fish sauce
1 tablespoon soy sauce
1 teaspoon granulated sugar
½ teaspoon salt

For the nage (broth):
1½ cups AleSmith Horny Devil
1 large fresh kaffir lime leaf
1 small shallot, peeled and
  sliced
1-inch piece fresh ginger, sliced
1 garlic clove, peeled, smashed

½ teaspoon whole coriander
  seed

For the fish:
½ bunch fresh cilantro, leaves
  picked (throw stems in nage)
4 scallions, cleaned, trimmed
1 lime
1½ pounds black cod, skin-on,
  cut into 4 equal portions
2 baby bok choy, halved
  lengthwise
1 package fresh maitake
  mushrooms, trimmed
20 Manila clams, rinsed

Finishing touch:
Steamed jasmine rice,
  optional

continued >

Schuyler likes to put his considerable talent to work with a good challenge, so he decided to create an original recipe just for this book. He wanted to use ingredients and a technique that others would not likely use — and here's the result. "It's a simple, highly aromatic steam-cooking recipe," Schuyler says. "You throw together all the flavors you want, and they all come together in the final dish."

ALESMITH'S HORNY DEVIL is a Belgian-style ale brewed with coriander, a flavor commonly used in Asian cuisine. Horny Devil has an array of spicy, floral notes that add extra layers of flavor to the dish and pair perfectly with fish. Recommended pairings: **HORNY DEVIL, DUVEL,** or **ORVAL.**

PERFECT PAIRING

STEAMED BLACK COD

continued from page 71

[PREPARATION]

1. Make the sauce: Combine all of the ingredients for the sauce in a medium bowl and set aside.

2. Make the nage: Combine all of the ingredients for the nage in a pot with a lid that can hold a wire steaming rack or fit below a bamboo steamer. Bring the mixture to a simmer.

3. Prepare the fish: Coarsely chop the cilantro leaves and slice the scallions very thin on the bias. Cut the lime in half, then cut one half into quarters and reserve the other half.

4. Score the skin side of the cod portions with ¼-inch-deep cuts approximately ½ inch apart. Season each portion on both sides with salt and place them on a plate or dish that will fit inside the steamer.

5. Arrange the baby bok choy halves, mushroom pieces, and clams around the cod pieces. If your steamer has multiple levels, like a traditional bamboo steamer, the fish may be on one level with the rest of the ingredients on a separate plate on another level. If you use this method, put the fish in the top level of the steamer.

6. Spoon the sauce over the cod portions, put everything into the steamer and close the lid. Steam for approximately 10 to 12 minutes, depending on the thickness of the fish.

7. When the fish is cooked through, the clams have opened, and the mushrooms and bok choy are tender, turn off the heat. Discard any unopened clams.

8. Arrange the bok choy and mushrooms in the centers of four wide bowls. Place the fish on top and divide the clams among the bowls.

9. Strain the nage and squeeze the reserved lime half into it. Pour the nage into the four bowls. Garnish each bowl with cilantro leaves, scallion, and a lime wedge. Serve with steamed jasmine rice, if desired.

Note: Wear gloves when chopping peppers, and avoid touching your eyes.

GINGER MUSSELS AND SOUR WENCH

COLBY CHANDLER, SPECIALTY BREWER, BALLAST POINT BREWING & SPIRITS   *[serves 8]*

Chef's Note: *There are many sour beers that can be substituted for the rare Sour Wench without Blackberries and the Hout Guezue. A great choice would be Ballast Point's Brother Levonian Saison or Wahoo Wheat. You lose some acidity when not using a sour beer, but a squeeze of lemon juice will provide some acid.*

4 tablespoons unsalted butter
10 ounces smoked thick-cut bacon,
  finely chopped
2 cups scallions, finely chopped
¼ cup fresh ginger, peeled and grated
4 cups Sour Wench without
  Blackberries
6 pounds Carlsbad Mussels,

bearded and rinsed
Ground black pepper, to taste
2 cups celery, tops of the stalks
  including leaves, finely chopped
2 cups heavy cream
2½ cups cilantro, finely chopped
  (divided use)
1 fresh baguette, sliced

[PREPARATION]

1. Melt the butter in a large pot over medium heat. Add the bacon and cook, stirring occasionally, for 10 to 20 minutes, or until brown.
2. Add the scallions and ginger, and simmer, stirring, for 4 minutes. Deglaze with ¼ cup of beer, add the mussels, and season with pepper.
3. Add the remaining beer, celery, and heavy cream, and cover the pot. Increase heat to high, bring to a boil, and steam the mussels until they open, about 3 to 6 minutes, depending on their size. Add 1½ cups of the cilantro and stir until well incorporated. Discard any mussels that do not open.
4. Divide the hot mussels into soup plates along with the broth. Garnish with the remaining cilantro and serve immediately with the baguette.

"This is a very simple dish that highlights fresh flavors from the sea and bright acidity from the beer," says Colby. "You want to get mussels that are as fresh as possible, and the the Sour Wench without Blackberries — a Berlinerweiss-style beer — will give you acidity for the sauce."

BALLAST POINT'S GUEZUE is an extraordinary beer, a truly special treat for lovers of sour beer. In an ideal world, this is the beer you would pair with the mussels, but it is not readily available to the public. "Our Gueuze-inspired ale is a blend of at least three different vintages of sour ale aged in used wine and bourbon oak barrels," Colby explains. "We only break it out for special events and anniversary parties." Any great sour without fruit would work well with this dish, and — if you desire less acidity — a Belgian-style wheat beer would also work beautifully.

PERFECT PAIRING

HEFEWEIZEN CORIANDER-BAKED SEA BASS
IN A TANGERINE-SCENTED REDUCTION WITH FRESH CORN AND TOMATO

RON OLIVER, CHEF DE CUISINE, THE MARINE ROOM   *[serves 4]*

The Marine Room is one of San Diego's renowned fine-dining restaurants, sitting literally on the sand of La Jolla Shores. Chef Ron Oliver, inspired by his surroundings, creates many seafood dishes. "I designed a dish for this book," Ron explains, "because I love to share recipes that are easy to prepare at home. I like the idea of pairing fresh ocean flavors with the crisp, mineral and effervescent qualities of beer."

For the fish:
1 tablespoon whole coriander seeds
1 tablespoon yellow mustard seeds
1 tablespoon grapeseed oil
4 (6-ounce) center-cut sea bass fillets, skinless, boneless
Sea salt and ground white pepper, to taste
Paprika to taste

1 tablespoon fresh dill, chopped
1 tablespoon fresh parsley, chopped
1 cup hefeweizen
1 tangerine, zested, juiced
2 tablespoons unsalted butter
2 cups fresh corn kernels
12 small cherry tomatoes, quartered

[PREPARATION]

1. Put coriander and mustard seeds in a small skillet over medium heat and cook, stirring constantly, until the mustard seeds start to pop and turn light brown. Transfer to a mortar and pestle or coffee grinder. Process until coarsely ground. Set aside.

2. Preheat oven to 350°F. Put the oil in an ovenproof skillet large enough to accommodate the sea bass fillets. Add sea bass, rolling in oil to coat. Season with salt and white pepper. Sprinkle toasted coriander mixture evenly over the top of the sea bass, allowing excess to fall around the fish into the skillet.

3. Sprinkle paprika, dill, and parsley evenly over the top of the fish, again allowing excess to fall into the skillet. Add beer, tangerine zest, and tangerine

continued >

PERFECT PAIRING

You'll want a great hefeweizen to drink with this dish. Ron loves **LIGHTNING'S THUNDERWEIZEN**, but you could go with **MISSION'S HEFEWEIZEN, CORONADO'S ORANGE AVENUE WIT, NEW ENGLISH WHY ? NOT**, or even a great Belgian-inspired wheat beer.

Ron says he chose to use hefeweizen because "it has aromatic qualities like coriander, clove, citrus, and even a little banana that complement the seasonings used on the fish."

juice to the skillet and put it in the oven. Bake until fish is flaky, but warm and translucent in the middle. (Time will vary depending on the thickness of fish, but as a guideline, cook for about 20 minutes for 1-inch-thick fillets.)

4. Remove the skillet from the oven and turn off heat. Using a slotted spatula, transfer the fish to an ovenproof dish and place it in the oven to keep warm.

5. Place the skillet on the stovetop over medium heat. Bring the liquid in the skillet to a boil, and add the corn kernels. Cook, stirring occasionally until the liquid is reduced by two-thirds. Turn off the heat and vigorously swirl in the butter. Fold in the tomatoes and season with salt and pepper.

6. Transfer the corn mixture to a large serving dish. Remove the sea bass from the oven and place it on top of the corn. Serve immediately.

BREWMASTER'S BEER-BATTERED FISH TACOS

JOHN EGAN, BREWMASTER, MISSION BREWERY   [serves 4]

John Egan is the brewmaster at Mission Brewery, one of San Diego's largest and fastest-growing breweries. Despite his hectic work schedule and all the pressures of a skyrocketing business, John needs to take time to chill — and a big part of his chill process is cooking. John knew he had the recipe down when he got rave reviews from relatives visiting from Sweden. If they don't know a good piece of fish, then who does?

For the batter:
12 ounces Mission Shipwrecked
    Double IPA (plus a bottle to drink
    while you're cooking!)
2 cups all-purpose flour
¾ teaspoon salt
1 teaspoon paprika
1 habanero pepper, very finely
    chopped*
1 egg

For the fish:
2 pounds fresh white fish, cut into
    2- to 3-inch strips (Giant White

Sea Bass is ideal, but cod,
    haddock, or halibut work well, too)
Salt and pepper
Vegetable oil, for frying
1½ cups all-purpose flour, for
    dusting fish before frying

Finishing touches:
8 flour or corn tortillas, warmed
Shredded cabbage
Your favorite Mexican white cream
    sauce
Fresh salsa
4 to 8 lime wedges

[PREPARATION]

1. Make the batter: Pour the beer slowly into a large bowl, and then sift in the flour, stirring as you go. Add the salt, paprika, and habanero. Whisk thoroughly while adding the egg until the mixture is nice and frothy. Set aside.

2. Prepare the fish: Lightly season both sides of the fish with salt and pepper.

continued >

PERFECT PAIRING

"An IPA would go well with this," John says, "but when I'm eating, I usually want something lighter, like a pilsner or a blonde. The really good IPAs (like **SHIPWRECKED**) are a little too heavy for me — they're almost a meal in themselves."

"I like fried food, like most dudes," John says. "I've made this recipe for a number of years, and I've always liked using IPAs in it. I love using Shipwrecked because it's got a great caramel sweetness but also bitterness."

3. Heat at least 2 inches of oil in a sauté pan to around 375°F. Toss a few pieces of the fish into the batter, then into to the flour, and then place in the frying pan. Fry to a golden brown, remove, and drain on a paper towel. Don't crowd the pan by frying too many pieces of fish at once.
4. For each taco, place a couple of pieces of fish on a tortilla and top with cabbage, white sauce, and salsa. Serve with lime wedges. Eat as soon as possible, while the batter is still hot and crispy!

*Note: Wear gloves when chopping the pepper, and avoid touching your eyes.

HESS BREWING'S GRAZIAS PARA PAELLA

MICHAEL SKUBIC, SALES MANAGER, HESS BREWING

[serves 4-6]

"The secret to making a great paella is the sofrito," says Mike Skubic. "You get a lot of flavor from cooking the onions and peppers in the same pan that has cooked the chicken and chorizo." Mike's other secret is the addition of beer to the cooking liquid, which adds a unique and delicious flavor to the dish.

For the saffron:
¼ cup of water
½ teaspoon or 2 pinches
    of saffron

For the chicken:
1 pound boneless, skinless
    chicken thighs, cut into 2-inch
    pieces
Kosher salt
Freshly ground black pepper
1 tablespoon paprika
½ cup extra-virgin olive oil
5 ounces dry-cured Spanish
    chorizo, cut into ¼-thick coins
1 red bell pepper, cut into ½-inch-
    thick strips
1 green bell pepper, cut into
    ½-inch-thick strips

For the *sofrito*:
1 yellow onion, minced
2 jalapeño peppers, seeded and
    chopped fine*
3 medium tomatoes, minced
3 cloves garlic, minced
½ teaspoon cayenne
    pepper

For the rice and broth:
2½ cups Valencia or bomba rice,
    (or any short-grain rice)
1 pound fresh peas
6 cups chicken broth
1 cup Grazias cream ale
12 giant prawns, peeled and
    deveined
12 mussels, rinsed and
    debearded

[PREPARATION]
1. Steep the saffron: Bring the water to a boil and take off the heat. Add the saffron and allow it to sit and steep until needed. **continued >**

PERFECT PAIRING

The subtle flavors of seafood, chicken, rice, and vegetables call for a beer that won't overpower. Hess's **GRAZIAS** (a cream ale) would work very nicely, as would a pale ale or a medium-malty red with a light hop character.

2. Cook the chicken: In a large bowl, toss the chicken pieces with the salt, pepper, and paprika to combine well.

3. In a large saucepan on high heat, get the olive oil very hot. Add the chicken and cook until pieces are cooked through (about 10 minutes). Remove the chicken from the pan and reserve.

4. To the pan, add the chorizo and the bell peppers and cook until peppers are lightly browned. Remove from the pan and set aside.

5. Cook the sofrito: With the pan back on high heat, add the onions and jalapeño peppers (add a bit more oil if needed) and cook for about 3 to 4 minutes. Add the tomatoes, garlic, and cayenne pepper and cook for another 1 to 2 minutes.

6. Prepare the rice: Add the rice and peas and cook with the sofrito for 2 more minutes. Once the rice is coated evenly, stop stirring and allow it to sit for about 1 minute. Add back the cooked chicken, chorizo, and peppers and mix to combine.

7. Prepare the beer and broth: In a medium pot, bring the chicken broth to a gentle simmer. Add the beer and the saffron liquid to the broth and pour into the pan with the rice. The rice should be covered in liquid. Cook, uncovered, for about 10 minutes without stirring.

8. When only a thin layer of cooking liquid remains, reduce the heat to medium and add the shrimp and mussels (be sure to place them hinge side down). Cook, uncovered, for 5 to 10 minutes, or until all the mussels have opened and the shrimp is opaque. Discard any mussels that do not open.

9. Turn off the heat and cover the pan for an additional 5 minutes. Then serve and enjoy.

Note: Wear gloves when chopping peppers, and avoid touching your eyes.

CALI BELGIQUE BRAISED PORK
WITH ORANGE AND FENNEL OVER JASMINE RICE

NICK BRUNE, EXECUTIVE CHEF, LOCAL HABIT

[serves 6-8]

"Springtime in Belgium." That's what Nick Brune of Local Habit credits as his inspiration for this dish. Braises in general are fairly easy to do, and this one is a simple combination of great flavors that all come together after hours on low heat. After you skim the fat from the braising liquid, you can reduce it to whatever consistency you desire before adding the pulled meat back to the sauce to coat.

5 pounds pork shoulder
Salt and pepper
¼ cup ground annatto
¼ cup peanut oil or canola oil
2 cups onion, chopped
⅓ cup garlic, chopped
¼ cup apple cider vinegar
4 cups Stone Cali Belgique (or other Belgian-style IPA)
4 large navel oranges
4 fennel bulbs, each cut into thirds
Olive oil
2 cups Jasmine rice

[PREPARATION]

1. Prepare the pork: Preheat oven to 325°F. Rinse the pork shoulder and pat it completely dry. Season well with salt and pepper and rub with the annatto.

2. Set the pork on a rack so the extra seasoning can fall off the pork. Let the shoulder rest for 10 minutes.

3. Heat a large, thick-bottomed ovenproof pot on medium-high heat for 2 minutes. Add the oil and place the pork shoulder in the pot, fat side down. Brown well, about 3 minutes per side.

4. Remove the pork and wipe out the remaining oil. Add the onions and garlic, stirring well, and cook for 2 minutes. Add the cider vinegar and continue to scrape the bottom of the pot, dissolving the

continued >

PERFECT PAIRING

The orange, fennel, and spice notes in this recipe help it to pair beautifully with a saison (**LOST ABBEY RED BARN ALE** or **IRON FIST'S HIRED HAND**) or a Belgian-style IPA — even a hefeweizen or dunkelweizen.

fonds (browned solids) that have developed. This should bring up more nice pork flavor.

5. Add the Cali Belgique, 1 orange cut in half, and the pork. Cover the pot with foil, and then put the lid on top to create a tight seal.

6. Place the pork in the oven and cook for 2½ hours.

7. While the pork is cooking, take the remaining 3 oranges and remove the skin, pith, membrane, and seeds. Separate into segments and set aside.

8. When pork is done, remove from the oven and let rest for 30 minutes. Do not remove the lid.

9. Preheat a grill on high. Once the pork has rested, remove the lid and pour all of the braising liquid into a clear container so you can see the rendered fat float to the top. Skim off and discard the fat.

10. Cook the jasmine rice (or preferred rice) according to package directions. While the rice is cooking, pull the meat from the bone. Remove fat and any tough portions. Put the pulled meat back into the braising liquid on the stove and heat on low.

11. Brush fennel bulbs with olive oil and salt and pepper to taste, and grill for 3 minutes on each side. To serve, place rice in a shallow bowl, top with the pork and then the grilled fennel, and finish with orange pieces.

CREOLE EGGS IN PURGATORY
WITH HOP BUTTER-FRIED EGGS, JAMBALAYA RISOTTO CAKES, CRAWFISH, SAUCE PIQUÁNT AND WORCESTERSHIRE PORTER REDUCTION

BRANDON HERNÁNDEZ, AWARD-WINNING FOOD-AND-BEER JOURNALIST *[serves 4]*

"This is a Creole-and-beer-infused take on an Italian breakfast/ brunch dish," Brandon explains. Laissez les bons temps rouler!

Chef's Note: *This recipe is best when started a full day in advance.*

For the Creole spice blend:
(Yield: about 1¼ cups)
¼ cup smoked paprika
¼ cup salt
2 tablespoons garlic powder
2 tablespoons onion powder
2 tablespoons ground dried oregano
2 tablespoons ground dried thyme
2 tablespoons freshly ground black pepper
1 tablespoon cayenne pepper

For the Worcestershire porter reduction:
1 cup Ballast Point Black Marlin Porter
½ cup Worcestershire sauce

For the hop butter:
½ cup unsalted butter
2½ tablespoons fresh Cascade hops
Salt, to taste

For the risotto:
2 cups chicken stock
2 tablespoons tomato sauce
¼ teaspoon Worcestershire sauce
3 tablespoons olive oil
½ cup Andouille sausage, finely diced
1 chicken thigh, boneless, skinless
Salt, to taste
2 tablespoons yellow onion, finely diced

continued >

PERFECT PAIRING

For pairing, you want a beer with enough hoppiness to cut the spice, but also a beer with enough richness to stand up to risotto and mouth-coating egg yolk. In Brandon's opinion, "There are few beers that simultaneously provide delicious malt and hop character as well as **ALESMITH'S ANVIL ESB**. It doesn't get the hype of their **SPEEDWAY STOUT** or **OLD NUMBSKULL**, but it shows just as much skillful craftsmanship and delivers a whole lot of flavor."

CREOLE EGGS IN PURGATORY
continued from page 84

2 tablespoons red bell pepper, finely diced
½ tablespoon celery, peeled and finely diced
½ tablespoon garlic, minced
¼ cup AleSmith Anvil ESB
¾ cup Arborio rice
Freshly ground black pepper to taste
Vegetable oil, for frying

For the sauce piquánt:
(Makes 4 cups)

2 tablespoons olive oil
½ cup yellow onion, diced
¼ cup red bell pepper, seeded and diced
2 tablespoons jalapeño pepper, seeded and diced*
Salt, to taste
2 tablespoons garlic, minced
2 teaspoons fresh thyme, finely chopped
1 teaspoon ground dried oregano
2 bay leaves
2 cups Roma tomatoes, peeled, seeded, and chopped
2 cups chicken stock
2 teaspoons vinegar-based hot sauce
¼ teaspoon freshly ground black pepper
2 tablespoons unsalted butter

For the fried eggs:
4 large eggs
Salt and freshly ground black pepper
¼ pound cooked crawfish tail meat

[PREPARATION]

1. Make the spice blend: Thoroughly combine all of the ingredients. Store in an airtight container.

2. Make the porter reduction: Combine the ingredients in a small saucepan over medium-high heat. Bring the mixture to a boil and reduce to a syrupy consistency. Let the mixture cool to room temperature before serving, or store, refrigerated, in an airtight container, for up to 10 days.

3. Make the hop butter: Melt the butter over medium-low heat in a small saucepan. Remove from heat and submerge the hops in the butter. Let stand for 20 minutes. Strain the butter into a condiment cup, using a spoon to mash out the butter that has been absorbed by the hops. Season the butter with salt and let stand until the butter cools to room temperature. Cover with plastic wrap and refrigerate until the butter solidifies. Store in an airtight container for up to 2 weeks.

4. Make the risotto: Combine the stock, tomato sauce, and Worcestershire sauce in a medium pot over medium-low heat and bring to a simmer. Reduce heat to low and keep warm.

5. Heat the olive oil in a large pot over medium heat. Add the Andouille and cook, stirring occasionally, until browned, 2 to 3 minutes. Remove the Andouille using a

continued >

Brandon Hernández:

"For the sauce, I use a traditional Louisianan sauce piquant with the sweet addition of crawfish meat. My favorite component is the risotto, prepared like a New Orleans jambalaya with Andouille sausage, blackened chicken, and "the trinity" — onion, celery and bell pepper."

slotted spoon and set aside.

6. Season the chicken with salt and 1 teaspoon of the spice blend, and add to the pot. Cook until golden brown, 5 to 6 minutes. Remove the chicken and set aside.

7. Add the onion, bell pepper, and celery to the pot, season with ½ teaspoon of spice blend and salt, and cook until tender, 2 to 3 minutes. Add the garlic and cook, stirring, for 1 minute. Add the beer, bring to a boil, and cook until reduced by two-thirds. Add the rice and cook, stirring, for 1 minute.

8. Use a ladle to add ¾ cup of liquid to the rice mixture and cook, stirring constantly, until most of the liquid has been absorbed. Repeat the process until the rice is cooked through, 25 to 30 minutes, being careful not to overcook. If more liquid is required, add additional stock, being sure to warm it before adding it to the rice. Chop the chicken into small pieces and fold it into the rice, along with the sausage. Transfer the risotto to a greased 13-by-9-inch baking dish, using a spatula to press it gently into an even layer. Let cool to room temperature, then cover with plastic wrap and refrigerate for at least 2 hours.

9. Make the sauce piquánt: Heat the oil in a large saucepan over medium-high heat. Add the onion, bell pepper, and jalapeño, season with salt, and cook, stirring occasionally, for 4 minutes. Add the garlic, thyme, oregano, and bay leaves, and cook, stirring, for 2 minutes. Add the tomatoes, stock, hot sauce, and pepper, and bring to a boil. Cook, stirring, for 2 minutes. Reduce heat to medium-low and simmer, stirring occasionally, for 5 minutes. Remove the bay leaves.

10. Transfer the mixture to the bowl of a blender or food processor and pulse until smooth. Return the mixture to the saucepan, reduce heat to low, and stir in the butter. Keep warm on low heat.

11. Remove the risotto dish from the refrigerator and use a 3-inch ring mold to cut out 4 cakes. Set aside and let the cakes return to room temperature.

12. Warm the sauce piquánt in a saucepan over medium-low heat. Reduce heat to low and keep warm.

13. Heat a thin layer of vegetable oil in a large, heavy-bottomed skillet over medium heat. Place the risotto cakes in the skillet and fry until golden brown, 1 to 2 minutes per side. Remove from the skillet and keep warm.

14. Melt the hop butter in a large skillet over medium heat. Crack the eggs into the skillet, season with salt and pepper, and fry until the whites are fully cooked, being careful not to overcook the yolks, 2 to 3 minutes. Remove the eggs from the skillet, and use the ring mold to cut out rounds from the eggs centered around the yolks.

15. Season the crawfish tails with salt and add to the skillet with any remaining hop butter. Cook until warmed through, about 1 minute. Remove from the heat and drain on paper towels.

16. To serve, spoon a ladleful of the sauce in the center of a bowl. Place a risotto cake in the center and top the cake with a fried egg. Spoon a drop of the reduction atop the egg yolk. Arrange several crawfish tails around the cake and serve immediately.

Note: Wear gloves when dicing peppers, and avoid touching your eyes.

BUNZ BURGER WITH SMOKED PORTER BACON JAM

JEFF ROSSMAN, CHEF/OWNER, BUNZ

[serves 4]

"*This is one of my newest burger toppings,*" *Jeff says proudly, speaking about his beer-bacon jam.* "*It's got a little smokiness, a little sweetness, a little citrus. It's one of my new favorites!*" *Jeff says,* "*You can use the beer-bacon jam for all kinds of grilled meats. And the Bunz sauce works for chicken, BLTs, even a turkey sandwich!*"

For the beer-bacon jam:
¼ pound uncooked bacon, cut in large dice
1½ cups onion, cut in small dice
½ jalapeño pepper, cut in small dice*
¼ tablespoon garlic, minced
1 teaspoon ground coriander
½ cup granulated sugar
12 ounces Stone Smoked Porter
½ teaspoon kosher salt
¼ teaspoon freshly ground black pepper
½ cup orange marmalade
½ tablespoon fresh thyme leaves

For the Bunz house sauce:
¾ cup mayonnaise
⅛ cup whole-grain mustard
3 tablespoons Heinz ketchup

1½ teaspoons Worcestershire sauce
¼ teaspoon garlic powder
¼ teaspoon ground cumin
¼ teaspoon chili powder

For the burgers:
1⅓ pounds ground beef (80 percent lean), divided into 4 patties
Salt and pepper
2 poblano chile peppers, roasted, seeded, and sliced
4 leaves romaine
8 slices tomato
8 slices red onion, separated into rings
4 whole-wheat burger buns (I love Bread & Cie)

[PREPARATION]
1. Make the jam: In a large saucepan on medium heat, fry the bacon until fully cooked. Remove the bacon and drain on paper towels,

continued >

PERFECT PAIRING

Because this dish has so many different flavor components — everything from smoky to sweet to fatty to spicy — you can decide which elements you want to complement and which you want to contrast. A light Kolsch-style pilsner or pale ale will contrast with the richness of the meat and the bacon, while a smoky porter or rausch-style beer will pump up the smoke component.

leaving the fat in the pan. In the same pan on medium-high heat, sauté the onion until caramelized, 15 to 20 minutes. Add jalapeño and garlic, and sauté for about 2 minutes, until tender. Add the remaining ingredients (except the thyme) and cook at a rolling boil for 10 to 15 minutes. Once the mixture has thickened, remove it from the heat and add the thyme and the cooked bacon pieces. Reserve.

2. Make the Bunz House sauce: Combine all the ingredients well in a bowl.

3. Preheat a grill on high.

4. Grill the burgers: Evenly salt and pepper each patty and grill to desired temperature.

5. Assemble the burgers: Toast the buns slightly on the grill. Add a little Bunz sauce to the bottom and top of each bun, and lay a patty on the bottom half of each bun. Lay some slices of poblano pepper, a piece of lettuce, 2 slices of tomato and 2 rings of onion on each burger. Top with 2 tablespoons bacon jam and the top of the bun.

Note: Wear gloves when dicing pepper, and avoid touching your eyes.

TORONADO'S ARRABIATA (ARRA•BEER•ATA)

NATE SOROKO, HEAD CHEF, TORONADO SAN DIEGO

[serves 4]

1 teaspoon olive oil
1 cup onion, chopped
1 large shallot, minced
5 cloves garlic, minced
½ cup red sour or kreik beer (I
   love Rodanbach or Red Poppy)
2 tablespoons honey
½ cup tomato paste
Pinch freshly ground
   black pepper

1½ teaspoons crushed red
   pepper
2 pounds Roma tomatoes, puréed
1 pound linguine (or spaghetti)
4 tablespoons butter

Finishing touches:
4 tablespoons fresh parsley,
   chopped
Freshly grated Parmesan cheese

[PREPARATION]

1. Put a pot of water on to boil (enough to cook a pound of pasta).
2. In large skillet or sauté pan, heat the oil to hot and sauté the onion, shallot, and garlic until translucent, about 6 minutes.
3. Stir in the beer, honey, tomato paste, black pepper, and red pepper flakes. Combine well.
4. Mix in the puréed tomatoes, bring to a boil, and reduce heat to medium. Simmer for 20 minutes, uncovered.
5. Cook linguine or spaghetti until al dente. Drain and add to sauté pan. Cook for 1 minute with sauce.
6. Just before serving, swirl in the butter to melt, add salt to taste, and sprinkle with parsley and freshly grated Parmesan cheese.

Even though the recipe uses a kreik-style beer ("**CUVEE DE TOMME** also works really well"), the spiciness of the dish makes it a good partner for an IPA, such as **GREEN FLASH'S WEST COAST IPA**, **PORT BREWING'S MONGO**, or **CORONADO'S ISLANDER** or **IDIOT IPA**.

PERFECT PAIRING

"I like simple dishes that feature a few great flavors and ingredients," Nate says. "Four or five ingredients is my ideal, usually." This recipe features tomatoes, spice, beer, and cheese. Nate said he noticed, when he was looking up recipes, that a classic arrabiata has red wine and vinegar in it. "I thought, wow! I could use Rodanbach or Red Poppy and omit the vinegar and red wine. With the beer, I'd get that sweetness and acidity at the same time!"

GINGHAM'S BEER-BRAISED LAMB SHANKS

RYAN STUDEBAKER, EXECUTIVE CHEF, GINGHAM   *[serves 8]*

Ryan Studebaker is the executive chef at Gingham, one of San Diego's newest and coolest restaurants. "Our focus is rustic American," Ryan explains. "We incorporate flavors from the South, with Cajun, Creole, and classic barbecue ingredients." The lamb, Ryan says, is his "French-influenced menu item for Gingham. Lamb is a popular meat on French menus, and the braise is a traditional cooking technique, but we added the chiles and the beer to give it our special touch and to bring it around to more of a barbecue-influenced kind of braise."

Chef's Note: *Begin this recipe a day in advance. The recipe can be cut in half to serve 4.*

8 lamb shanks
Salt and freshly ground black
   pepper
1 bunch fresh thyme
1 orange, zested and juiced
1 to 3 Fresno chiles, minced,
   to taste
6 tablespoons canola oil or
   vegetable oil, divided use
¾ cup garlic, smashed
½ cup tomato paste
8 cups mirepoix (carrots, celery,
   and onion cut in large dice)

24 ounces hefeweizen (or other
   wheat beer)
¾ cup fresh-squeezed orange
   juice
16 cups chicken stock
16 cups vegetable stock

Finishing touches:
Gremolata (4 tablespoons
   chopped parsley, 2 tablespoons
   chopped garlic, and 2
   tablespoons orange zest)

[PREPARATION]

1. Season the lamb shanks with salt, pepper, thyme, orange zest, chiles, and 4 tablespoons of vegetable oil. Cover and refrigerate overnight.
2. Preheat oven to 300°F.
3. Wipe the herbs, orange, and chiles from the shanks and reserve. In a large sauté pan, heat the remaining oil to hot and sear the shanks on all sides. As each is seared, place it in a large ovenproof roasting pan.

continued >

PERFECT PAIRING

"I love to use **BLACK MARKET'S HEF** for this dish," Ryan explains. "It's got a lot of citrus and orange flavors that accent the lamb beautifully." Other great wheat-beer choices would be **CORONADO'S ORANGE AVENUE WIT**, **HANGAR 24 ORANGE WIT**, or **MISSION HEFEWEIZEN**.

4. Add the mirepoix to the sauté pan and cook until the vegetables are browned and caramelized, 10 to 15 minutes.

5. Add the garlic to the pan and cook until softened but not browned. Stir in the tomato paste and sauté briefly.

6. Add the beer and orange juice, and simmer until reduced by one-third. Pour the mirepoix mixture into a large stockpot, add the stocks, and bring to a boil.

7. Pour the liquid into the roasting pan to cover the lamb. Cover with foil or parchment paper and cook in the oven for 3 hours, or until the meat is fork-tender and pulls away easily from the bone. Serve topped with gremolata and a starch of your choice. (Grits make a good accompaniment).

TIGER! TIGER! BRATWURST

AARON LAMONICA, EXECUTIVE CHEF, TIGER! TIGER!
AND BLIND LADY ALE HOUSE

[makes 30 sausages]

*Chef Aaron LaMonica —
and the other folks at Blind
Lady Ale House and Tiger!
Tiger! — are constantly
surrounded by a huge variety
of great beer. That may be
why they are on a mission to
create food that pairs perfectly
with beer. Needless to say, a
great brat and a great beer
are a match made in heaven.
This is Chef Aaron's "go-
to" brat recipe, and it also
happens to be one of his best-
selling menu items.*

Chef's Note: Insta Cure No. 1 is a nitrate — a preservative that also maintains the color of cured meats. You can find it at sausage-making specialty sites online as well as in San Diego at Iowa Meat Farms. You can omit this ingredient, but the color and shelf-life of the sausages will be affected. With Insta Cure, they will last refrigerated for up to 2 weeks; without, they will oxidize in about 3 days. Either way, they can be frozen for up to 3 months.

6 pounds pork shoulder, fat trimmed,
   diced for grinding
3 pounds pork back fat, diced for
   grinding
4 tablespoons salt
8 ounces dry milk powder
2 tablespoons white pepper
4½ teaspoons ground ginger
4½ teaspoons mace
4 tablespoons ground coriander

4 teaspoons Insta Cure No. 1
1¼ teaspoons ground cardamom
½ cup fresh marjoram, chopped
2½ tablespoons garlic, minced
2½ teaspoons celery seed
3 large eggs
1½ cups heavy cream
35-mm hog casings, approximately
   25 to 30 feet (available at Iowa
   Meat Farms)

[PREPARATION]

1. Chill the meat and fat in separate bowls for a minimum of 2 hours, or until very cold. Grind the meat and return to refrigerator. Grind the fat and return to the refrigerator.

2. In a medium bowl, mix all the dry ingredients together well. **continued >**

PERFECT PAIRING

The great thing about brats is that you can pair them with nearly any kind of beer. The traditional German bratwurst is, of course, paired with the traditional German-style pilsners and lagers. But a lot will depend on your toppings: If you go spicy, you may want an IPA or a black IPA; if you go sweet, you may want a malt-forward beer, such as a red ale or a brown.

3. In a small bowl, whisk together the eggs and cream.

4. In a large mixer bowl, mix the meat, fat, and spices together, and add the egg-and-cream mixture. Mix well on low- to medium-speed. Return the mixture to the refrigerator to chill completely (about 2 hours).

5. Rinse the casings and pat dry.

6. With the sausage stuffing attachment on a mixer or grinder, stuff the casings. Refrigerate until ready to use.

7. Preheat a grill to medium-high. Heat pot of water or beer on the stove to a temperature of 165°F and drop in the sausages. Poach the sausages until they are firm and the internal temperature reaches 140°F. Finish cooking the sausages on the grill.

THREE LI'L PIGS BURGER
(PULLED PORK, BACON, AND HAM WITH BEER-THYME MUSTARD)

JEFF ROSSMAN, CHEF/OWNER BUNZ

[serves 4]

Like most San Diego beer fans, Chef Jeff Rossman knows that having pork and beer together is one of the carnivore's greatest pleasures. So, why not go for it? "This burger is an in-your-face, unabashed pork-lover's dream," Jeff says. "And the combination of pork three different ways makes this dish a really fun combination of textures and flavors."

Chef's Note: *Start the mustard preparation and pork a day ahead.*

For the mustard:
1⅓ cups black mustard seeds
2 cups Karl Strauss Amber (or your favorite beer)
1½ cups malt vinegar
⅓ teaspoon ground allspice
⅔ teaspoon ground black pepper
2 teaspoons kosher salt
4 teaspoons granulated sugar
⅛ cup dry mustard
1¼ tablespoons garlic, minced
⅛ cup horseradish
⅛ cup fresh thyme leaves, chopped

For the pulled pork:
3 pounds pork butt
Salt and pepper
1 yellow onion, cut into eighths
1 carrot, cut into 2-inch dice
1 celery stalk, cut into 2-inch dice
1 Gala apple, cut into quarters

12 cloves garlic
3 sprigs mixed herbs
1 tablespoon star anise
1 cinnamon stick
36 ounces beer (any favorite not-too-hoppy brew will do)
1 cup apple juice

For the burger:
2 onions, cut into 1-inch slices
1 tablespoon canola oil
1⅓ pounds ground beef (80 percent lean), made into 4 patties
8 slices cooked bacon
4 slices ham
4 (1-ounce) sharp cheddar cheese slices
4 whole-wheat burger buns (I love Bread & Cie)
4 leaves romaine
8 slices tomato

continued >

PERFECT PAIRING

Jeff loves cooking with (and drinking) **KARL STRAUSS AMBER,** so he recommends pairing it with this burger as well. With this many flavors and components, almost any type of golden-colored to light-red beer with good hop acidity will tie your meal together successfully.

[PREPARATION]

1. Start the mustard: In a small bowl, combine the mustard seeds, beer, and malt vinegar. Cover and soak overnight.

2. Preheat oven to 375°F.

3. Prepare the pork: Cut the meat into 3 or 4 smaller pieces and season with salt and pepper. Heat a sauté pan and sear the pork on each side for 3 minutes. Remove the pork from the pan. Sauté the onion, carrot, celery, and apple (add a little olive oil if needed) for about 2 minutes and then add the garlic and herbs. In a casserole dish, combine the sautéed vegetables with the star anise, cinnamon stick, beer, and apple juice. Place the pork in the dish on top of the vegetable mix. Cover with foil and bake for about 3 hours, or until the meat is fork-tender and begins to fall away when poked. Remove the pork from the dish, strain the liquid, and cool. When the pork is cool enough to handle, pull it apart with a fork and refrigerate until needed. Chill the braising liquid overnight so the fat solidifies on top.

4. Remove the fat solids from the chilled braising liquid and discard. Combine some of the liquid with the pulled pork and reheat in a medium pan. Season with salt and pepper.

5. Finish the mustard: Strain and reserve the beer-vinegar liquid in a separate container. Place the soaked mustard seeds in a blender and purée for about 20 seconds, until most of the seeds are cracked. In a double boiler on medium heat, combine the cracked seeds with the allspice, pepper, salt, sugar, dry mustard, garlic, and horseradish, and the vinegar-beer liquid. Cook about 1 hour, stirring occasionally. Remove from heat and cool. Add thyme leaves and refrigerate.

6. Preheat a grill on high heat.

7. Prepare the burgers: In a mixing bowl, toss the onion slices with the oil, season with salt and pepper, and grill.

8. Grill the burgers: Salt and pepper each patty, and grill to desired temperature. Finish on grill by adding

3 ounces of pulled pork, 2 slices of bacon, 1 slice of ham, and 1 ounce of cheese to each burger. Allow the toppings to heat and melt before removing the burger from the grill.

9. Assemble the burgers: Toast the buns slightly and spread a little mustard on the bottom and tops of each. Lay each patty (with the goods) on the bottom of a bun. Top with a piece of lettuce, 2 slices of tomato, and some grilled onion. Top with other half of the bun and dig in!

PORK STOUT OSSO BUCO

BRIAN MURPHY, EXECUTIVE CHEF, RIVIERA SUPPER CLUB *[serves 6]*

Chef Brian Murphy (right, with co-owner Tim Mays) of Riviera Supper Club has very fond memories of AleSmith's early days, when Speedway Stout was relatively new and Charlie Upham brought the first keg to Live Wire Bar. "I've loved Speedway ever since," Brian admits. "It's got such intense flavor, and it's bold. That's why I love how this recipe combines the chocolate and coffee and sweetness with bold spices and heat from chiles."

For the rub:
¾ cup smoked paprika
¼ cup freshly ground black pepper
¼ cup sea salt
⅛ cup granulated sugar
2 tablespoons California chili powder (made with dried Anaheim chiles)
2 tablespoons garlic powder
2 tablespoons onion powder
1 teaspoon cayenne pepper

For the pork:
2 tablespoons canola oil or grapeseed oil
½ cup carrots, coarsely chopped
½ cup celery, coarsely chopped
½ cup onion, coarsely chopped
6 whole cloves garlic
6 (12- to 16-ounce) pork shanks

4 cups of AleSmith Speedway Stout

For the sauce:
¼ cup strained braising liquid
¼ cup AleSmith Speedway Stout
2 tablespoons Worcestershire sauce
2 cups of your favorite top-quality bottled barbecue sauce
2 limes, juiced
2 tablespoons prepared chipotle hot sauce (I like Bufalo brand)

For the gremolata:
1 tablespoon cilantro, finely chopped
1 tablespoon lime zest, finely chopped
½ teaspoon garlic, finely chopped

[PREPARATION]
1. Preheat oven to 450°F. In a bowl, mix together the rub ingredients. Coat the entire bottom and sides of a medium heavy-duty Dutch oven

continued >

PERFECT PAIRING

Though **SPEEDWAY** makes an excellent addition to the flavors of this dish, it may be a little heavy to drink as an accompaniment. A malty beer with more up-front hoppiness would likely be the best companion: **GREEN FLASH'S HOP HEAD RED, AZTEC'S SACRIFICE RED IPA,** and **ALESMITH'S NAUTICAL NUT BROWN** are prime examples.

with oil. (The pot should be just wide enough to hold all 6 shanks. If it is larger, you will need more liquid for braising.) Line the bottom of the pot with carrots, celery, onion, and whole garlic cloves.

2. Coat pork shanks generously with the rub and stand them up on top of the vegetables in the prepared Dutch oven. Put the pot into the center of the oven and allow the shanks to sear for about 15 minutes. Check to be sure they have seared, but don't let the spices burn.

3. Once the meat has seared, working quickly, add enough Speedway Stout to almost cover the shanks. Lower the heat to 375°F and return the pot to the oven for another 2½ to 3 hours, depending on the size of the shanks.

4. Make the gremolata: In a small bowl, combine the ingredients and set aside.

5. When the shanks are done, the meat should be ready to fall off the bone. Remove the pot from the oven and crank the heat up to broil.

6. Transfer the shanks to a platter, cover loosely with foil, and allow them to rest while you finish the sauce. Strain the braising liquid and measure out ¼ cup.

7. Make the sauce: Combine the strained braising liquid, Speedway Stout, Worcestershire sauce, barbecue sauce, and lime juice. Add enough chipotle hot sauce to your liking — you should taste a nice balance of sweet stout and spicy chiles in the tang of the sauce.

8. Baste each pork shank carefully with the sauce, trying not to sauce the bone. Lightly oil a baking sheet and place the shanks evenly spaced on the baking sheet. Once the broiler is hot, put the shanks under the broiler for 1 to 3 minutes, or until the sauce sets up and begins to crisp on the sides. Remove from the heat and serve with more sauce and a little gremolata sprinkled on top.

VELVET GLOVE MAC 'N' CHEESE

MIKE CAMPBELL, OPERATIONS MANAGER, IRON FIST BREWING CO.   *[serves 4-6]*

"The initial inspiration for this recipe actually came from my wife, Melody," Mike Campbell (right, with Brandon Sieminski) explains. "She encouraged me to keep it simple but do something with a little twist. She's always loved my mac 'n' cheese, but I had never done it with beer. So, I went to Brandon (Iron Fist's brewmaster and boy genius), and he had one word for me: 'stout.' So that's what we did."

4 cups heavy cream
5 strips bacon
8 ounces crumbled pork sausage
1 stick unsalted butter
½ cup all-purpose flour
1 cup Iron Fist Velvet Glove Imperial Oatmeal Stout
14 ounces extra-sharp white cheddar cheese, cut up or grated
8 ounces Gruyere cheese, cut up or grated
½ tablespoon freshly ground black pepper
½ tablespoon salt
1-pound package elbow noodles, cooked and drained
2 cups sourdough bread crumbs or crushed croutons
1 fresh jalapeño pepper, thinly sliced* (optional)
Sriracha hot sauce, to taste

[PREPARATION]

1. Preheat oven to 375°F. In a small saucepan, heat the heavy cream until just warm (not boiling).
2. In a large skillet, cook the bacon and sausage together until crispy and brown. Remove and set aside, reserving the grease in the skillet.
3. In the skillet with the bacon greas, melt the butter over low heat. Slowly add flour and whisk together until smooth. Cook for 2 minutes.
4. Slowly add the warm heavy cream and the beer, bring to a low boil, and cook until thick and creamy, approximately 1 to 2 more minutes. Remove from heat.
5. With the skillet off the heat, add the cheddar, Gruyere, pepper, and salt.

continued >

PERFECT PAIRING

The entire Iron Fist lineup boasts exceptionally food-friendly Belgian-inspired beers (maybe it's Brandon Sieminski's culinary training), so there's no need to look beyond **IRON FIST'S SPICE OF LIFE** (Belgian-style spiced ale), **RENEGADE BLONDE** (Kolsch-style blonde ale) or **HIRED HAND** (saison) for a great pairing.

Return to the heat and stir until the cheese is completely melted. Add the bacon and sausage and mix together.

6. In a large baking dish, put half of the drained pasta and half of the cheese mixture and blend together. On top of that, add the rest of the pasta and the cheese mixure. Blend together and sprinkle the top with bread crumbs.

7. Bake for 30 to 40 minutes, until hot throughout and the bread crumbs are lightly browned.

8. Garnish with sliced jalapeño, if desired, and drizzle with Sriracha to taste.

Note: Wear gloves when slicing peppers, and avoid touching your eyes.

SOUR WENCH-BRAISED DUCK
WITH SMASHED SAVORY YAMS AND GARLICKY GREENS

TYSON BLAKE, GENERAL MANAGER, O'BRIEN'S PUB

[serves 4]

For the duck:
8 large duck legs
Salt and freshly ground black
    pepper, to taste
2 cups Ballast Point Sour Wench
    (or another fruity lambic)
¼ cup granulated sugar (omit if
    using a sweeter fruit lambic)
1 cup dried tart cherries
1 large yellow onion, chopped
2 heads garlic, cloves separated
    and peeled
3 sprigs fresh thyme
4 cups chicken broth
1 (8-ounce package) fresh
    blackberries
2 tablespoons chives, finely
    chopped

For the yams:
¼ cup extra-virgin olive oil
2 tablespoon garlic powder
1 tablespoon kosher salt
2 teaspoons dried sage
4 large yams, peeled and cut
    into ¼-inch-thick rounds
½ stick salted butter, softened
¾ cup whole milk
Salt and freshly ground black
    pepper, to taste

For the greens:
2 tablespoons extra-virgin
    olive oil
4 bunches spinach, cleaned
    and trimmed
Salt and freshly ground black
    pepper, to taste
4 cloves garlic, finely chopped

continued >

Tyson Blake (left, with O'Brien's owner Tom Nickel) is a hardcore duck lover, so he's always thinking about new ways to prepare the bird. Tyson is also a hardcore Ballast Point fan, so pairing a BP beer with duck is his idea of heaven. "Sour Wench is always a treat when it comes out," Tyson says. "It's a really tart beer made with blackberries, so it's automatically a natural for pairing with something fatty."

BALLAST POINT'S SOUR WENCH is a Belgian lambic-style ale brewed with blackberries, but it's also similar to a *Berlinerweiss*. It has an array of fruity notes, low bitterness, and a high acidity that cuts through fattiness and adds brightness to the dish. Recommended pairing: Sour Wench or other lambic-style beer.

PERFECT PAIRING

SOUR WENCH-BRAISED DUCK

continued from page 103

[PREPARATION]

1. **Prepare the duck:** Preheat oven to 350°F. Season the duck legs with salt and pepper, and put them in a heavy ovenproof pot just large enough to hold them in one layer. Cook the legs, skin side down, on the stovetop over moderate heat for 10 to 15 minutes, or until the skin is golden and crisp. (The duck doesn't have to be perfectly crisp because you will finish it later in the broiler). Turn the legs over and cook until lightly browned on the other side, about 2 minutes. Transfer the legs to a plate and set aside. Reserve the fat from the pan.

2. Pour the beer into the pan. Whisk in the sugar and a pinch of salt. Use a wooden spoon to scrape the brown bits from the bottom of the pot. Bring the beer to a boil and cook until the mixture has reduced by half. Add the cherries, onion, garlic, and thyme. Return the duck legs, skin side up, to the pot and add the broth. Bring the mixture to a simmer. Then cover the pot and place it in the oven. Braise the duck for 2 hours, or until the meat is fork-tender.

3. **Prepare the yams:** Combine the oil, garlic powder, salt, and sage in a zipper-top plastic bag. Seal the bag and shake vigorously to combine. Place the yams in the marinade and let sit for 1 hour.

4. Bring a grill or grill pan to high heat, about 450°F. Add the yams and grill until they are cooked though and lightly charred, about 2 to 3 minutes per side. Place the yams in a pot on low heat. Add the butter and use a potato masher to smash the yams. When the butter is completely incorporated, add the milk and smash until the mixture is fairly smooth with chunks throughout. Season with salt and pepper to taste and set aside until ready to serve.

5. **Make the greens:** Heat the oil in a large pan over high heat. When the oil starts to smoke, add the spinach. Season with salt and pepper and cook, gently and continuously tossing with tongs, until the spinach is wilted, about 2 minutes. Add the garlic and cook for 1 minute. Re-season with salt and pepper as needed and set aside until ready to serve.

6. When duck legs are done, transfer them, skin side up, to a sheet pan and cover with aluminum foil to keep warm. Set the oven to broil and position the oven rack in the upper third of the oven.

7. Pour the braising mixture into a 1-quart measuring cup and let stand until the fat rises to the top. Skim off the fat and strain the liquid through a sieve into a saucepan over medium-high heat, pressing hard on the solids to release all of the liquid.

8. Add half of the blackberries and bring the mixture to a boil. Cook until the liquid has reduced by about one-third and has slightly thickened. Lower the heat and simmer the mixture for about 5 minutes. Season with salt and pepper as needed. Remove from heat and add the remaining blackberries.

9. Place the duck legs in the oven, uncovered, and broil until the skin is crispy, about 2 minutes.

10. To serve, place some sweet potatoes and greens on each plate. Place 2 duck legs atop the vegetables, top with sauce and chives, and serve immediately.

LIGHTNING PULLED PORK SANDWICHES
WITH SWEET-AND-SOUR COLE SLAW

JIM CRUTE, FOUNDER, PRESIDENT, AND HEAD BREWER, LIGHTNING BREWERY
AND BILL WARNKE, PROFESSIONAL CHEF

[serves 8-10]

Chef's Notes: *This recipe requires making a sweet wort ahead of time and is best begun a day or two in advance. Pale malted 2-row barley is available at homebrew shops or from a friend who homebrews. As an alternative to the wort, obtain 1 pound light dried malt extract or 1¼ pounds light malt syrup from your local homebrew or health food store. Dissolve in 2 quarts of warm water. Bring to a boil, simmer for 20 minutes, and cool.*

For the traditional wort:
2 pounds pale malted 2-row barley
3 quarts water

For the braise:
4- to 5-pound pork shoulder or butt
Salt
1 cup chicken stock
1 large carrot, coarsely chopped
1 medium onion, coarsely chopped
1 to 2 ribs celery, coarsely chopped
2 garlic cloves, crushed, not minced
2 bay leaves
10 whole peppercorns

For the cole slaw:
⅓ cup granulated sugar
½ teaspoon ground celery or
　　cumin (or a mix of both)
1 teaspoon dry mustard
1 teaspoon salt
¼ teaspoon black pepper
⅓ cup cider or distilled vinegar
⅔ cup olive oil
½ green cabbage, shredded
½ red cabbage, shredded
1 medium red onion, diced
1 red jalapeño pepper, seeded
　　and finely diced*

continued >

One day, while Bill Warnke (right), a chef by trade, was working around the Lightning Brewery, he decided to get a taste of what brewer Jim Crute (left) kept referring to as "sweet wort." As soon as he tasted it, Bill knew he could do great things cooking with it. Bill realized that a sweet wort — lacking the bitterness of hops — can be added to dishes, used as a braising liquid, or even reduced to a molasses-type consistency, which is what they did to create the Lightning Sauce used in this recipe.

These sandwiches are best served with **LIGHTNING ELEMENTAL PILSNER**. The bitterness of the beer cuts through the malty sweetness of the braised pork, the yeastiness of the roll, and the richness of the sauce. Alternatively, a clean-tasting, medium-hoppy IPA like **LIGHTNING'S FAIR WEATHER PALE ALE** would work well.

PERFECT PAIRING

Jim Crute: "Sweet wort is high in umami, which typically acts as a flavor enhancer. That's another reason it's so great to cook with."

LIGHTNING PULLED PORK SANDWICHES

continued from page 105

For the sauce:

3 cups canned tomato purée (or whole canned tomatoes puréed in a food processor or blender)

2 cups granulated sugar

1 cup clover honey

⅓ cup cider vinegar

3 teaspoons freshly squeezed lemon juice

2 teaspoons dark brown sugar

2 teaspoons Worcestershire sauce

2 teaspoons soy sauce

1½ teaspoons kosher salt

1 teaspoon garlic powder

1 teaspoon onion powder

1 teaspoon Tabasco sauce

½ teaspoon ground black pepper

¼ teaspoon ground cloves

Finishing touch:

Crusty rolls

[PREPARATION]

1. Make the wort: Mill the grain with a grain mill, or grind it in a food processor or blender. The grains should just be cracked and not ground to the consistency of flour.

2. Heat 3 quarts of tap water to 100°F. Add the milled grain and heat to 120°F while stirring. Turn off the heat and allow to sit, covered, for 30 minutes. Reheat to 140°F while stirring and then allow to sit, covered, for 45 minutes. Reheat to 170°F and strain. Return the liquid to the pan and bring to a boil. Continue at a moderate boil for 20 to 30 minutes, uncovered,

until reduced by one-third. There should be about 2 quarts of sweet wort remaining. Set aside or cover and transfer to the refrigerator to cool. (If you don't use it immediately, it can be refrigerated for several days.)

3. Preheat oven to 300°F.

4. Prepare the pork: Wash, pat dry, and lightly salt the meat.

5. Place the pork in a roasting pan, add 2 cups of wort and all the ingredients for the braise, cover, and place in the oven for 3 to 3½ hours. The pork will be fork-tender and will fall apart when fully cooked.

6. Make the cole slaw: In a small saucepan, combine the sugar and seasonings. Gradually whisk in the vinegar and oil, and bring the mixture to a boil. Cook for 1 minute.

7. Combine the cabbage, onion, and jalapeño in a medium bowl. Pour the hot dressing over the cabbage mixture and toss well. Set aside.

8. Make the sauce: In a medium saucepan, boil 2 cups of wort until reduced to ¼ cup (or use ¼ cup of prepared and reduced malt extract liquid). Whisk together all of the sauce ingredients and add to the reduced wort. Heat to a boil and stir until the mixture thickens, about 10 minutes.

9. After braising the pork, remove the bone and separate the meat into medium-sized pieces, pull apart, and add to a slow-cooker or pan to keep warm. If desired, store in the refrigerator and warm before serving.

10. Assemble the sandwich: Cut each roll in half and toast, if desired. Add a portion of pulled pork, cover in sauce, and top with cole slaw.

Note: Wear gloves when dicing peppers, and avoid touching your eyes.

CHRIS GORT'S BREWER'S FLATBREAD PIZZA & PIZZA WITH BACON & SOUR CREAM TOPPING

CHRISTOPHER GORT, HEAD BREWER, BACK STREET BREWERY

[serves 4–6]

Back Street brewer Chris Gort says this pizza crust recipe was inspired by a trip he took with his wife to Potsdam, Germany, where one of the signature items is Flammkuchen, *a brick-oven-style pizza. After sampling* Flammkuchen, *Chris created a dough of his own. Being a brewer, he was, of course, inspired to put beer in the dough. He likes to use hefeweizen or a similar style wheat beer, since the bitterness is low and the wheatiness adds a special layer of flavor.*

For the flatbread pizza dough:
2 cups bread flour
2½ tablespoons olive oil
⅔ cup hefeweizen or other beer
    with low IBUs
1 pinch or more salt

For the topping:
8 to 12 small-to-medium Campari tomatoes or similar, sliced thin
½ cup balsamic vinegar
10 tablespoons olive oil
Salt and pepper, to taste
6 cloves garlic, minced
4 to 6 cups mozzarella cheese, shredded
6 ounces crumbled goat cheese
¼ cup honey

[PREPARATION]

1. Make the dough: In a large mixing bowl, combine the ingredients for the dough.

2. Mix until you can begin to knead the dough. Knead until the dough does not easily tear. Cover and leave the dough to rest for 30 minutes.

3. Preheat oven to 450°F.

4. Prepare the tomatoes for the topping: Place the tomatoes in a bowl and marinate in the balsamic vinegar. Set aside.

5. Once the dough has rested, cut it into quarters. Form each piece into a ball and roll each out, using a little more flour if needed, to about ⅛-inch thick.

continued >

PERFECT PAIRING

Depending on which toppings you use, different beers will shine. The sweetness of the honey and tomatoes would work nicely with everything from a crisp pilsner-style beer all the way to a hoppy IPA. If you go with the bacon topping, you could pair a hoppy red or go with an IPA to cut through the fattiness of the bacon and sour cream.

6. Put the dough rounds on oiled baking sheets with 2 pizzas per sheet.

7. Divide toppings into four portions each. Cover each pizza with oil, salt, pepper, and minced garlic. Add the mozzarella and the marinated tomato slices. Add the crumbled goat cheese, then drizzle honey generously over each pizza.

8. Bake until crust is golden brown and crispy, about 10 to 15 minutes. Let cool a few minutes before serving.

For the pizza with bacon and sour cream topping:

1 (16-ounce) container sour cream or Greek yogurt
½ pound bacon, cut into 1½-inch pieces and
    cooked crisp
Freshly ground black pepper, to taste
Grated lemon zest, to taste
2 tablespoons vegetable oil
1 large red onion, quartered and sliced
1 bunch green onions, chopped

[PREPARATION]

1. Make the dough: Follow the previous directions for making the dough.

2. Make the sauce: In a small bowl, combine the bacon and the sour cream or yogurt. Stir in the pepper and lemon zest. Dilute the sauce with a few drops of water, if needed.

3. In a skillet over medium-low heat, heat the oil and sauté the red onion until golden. You can add some bacon grease to the skillet if you like.

4. Roll out the dough according to the previous directions. Spread some of the sauce over each dough round.

5. Top with sautéed red onion and chopped green onion.

6. Bake until crust is golden brown and crispy, about 10 to 15 minutes. Let cool a few minutes before serving.

COWBOY CHICKEN SANDWICH
WITH BEER BATTER ONION RINGS AND STONE SMOKED PORTER BBQ SAUCE

JEFF ROSSMAN, CHEF/OWNER BUNZ

[serves 4]

"A smoky beer adds so much depth of flavor to a barbecue sauce," Chef Jeff Rossman says. *"The smokiness of a smoked porter also adds a dark, rich, luscious component that really makes it sing."* Jeff likes to use his special BBQ sauce on a host of dishes, including this chicken sandwich. The sauce, as you may imagine, is also great on a burger, ribs, or a delicious steak. *"I can put barbecue sauce on just about anything,"* Jeff says. *"It's one of those magical sauces that make everything taste good."*

For the BBQ sauce:
1 tablespoon canola oil
⅔ cup yellow onion, chopped
⅓ cup garlic, minced
2 teaspoons coriander seed, toasted and ground
1 teaspoon smoked paprika
1 teaspoon cayenne pepper
2¾ cups Stone Smoked Porter or any dark beer you like
1 ancho chile, rehydrated with 1 cup hot water
1 lime, zested
4⅓ cups ketchup, your favorite brand
½ bunch cilantro
⅔ cup molasses
½ cup rice wine vinegar
¼ cup brown sugar
1 teaspoon kosher salt

For the onion rings:
2½ cups all-purpose flour, divided use
2 teaspoons dried parsley
2 teaspoons garlic powder
1 teaspoon cumin
1 teaspoon chili powder
1 teaspoon dried chipotle chile, ground
2 teaspoons smoked paprika
1 tablespoon kosher salt
1 egg, beaten
12 ounces light blonde, lager, or kolsch-style beer
2 to 3 large yellow onions, sliced into thick rings
2 cups oil, for frying

For the chicken:
4 large boneless chicken thighs

continued >

PERFECT PAIRING

Light and crisp are the key concepts for pairing with this recipe. The BBQ sauce is rich and spicy, and the onion rings are fried and battered, so a clean, crisp beer with whatever hop profile you prefer — from low to high — will work nicely to balance the flavors that all come together here.

Salt and freshly ground black pepper
4 ounces sharp cheddar cheese slices
2 poblano chile peppers, roasted and seeded
8 slices cooked bacon
4 leaves romaine
8 slices tomato
4 whole-wheat burger buns (Bread & Cie is great)
4 large skewers

[PREPARATION]

1. Make the BBQ sauce: In a medium saucepan on high heat, heat the oil and sauté the onion for about 3 minutes. Lower the heat and add the garlic. Cook onion and garlic for another 3 minutes and then add dried spices. Add the remaining ingredients, bring to a boil, lower heat, and simmer for about 2 hours. Remove from heat and set aside.

2. Prepare the onion rings: In shallow bowl combine 2 cups of the flour with the dried parsley, garlic powder, cumin, chile powder, chipotle, paprika, and salt. In a separate bowl, mix together the beaten egg and beer. Gradually stir the beer mixture into the flour mixture, stirring until a thick batter forms. (Add more beer if the batter is too thick.)

3. Grill the chicken: Evenly salt and pepper each thigh and cook on the grill. Melt 1 ounce of cheese on each thigh before removing from the grill.

4. In a heavy frying pan or cast-iron skillet, heat the oil over medium-high heat. (Adjust the amount, depending on the size of your pan, so that you have a couple of inches of oil.) Drop the onions into a bowl of water, then toss them in a bowl with the ½ cup of flour. When the oil is hot (350° to 375°F), dip the onions in batter, shake off the excess, and fry, turning once to brown evenly on both sides. Drain on paper towels.

5. Assemble the sandwiches: Toast the buns slightly, and spread a little BBQ sauce on the bottom and top of each bun. Place a thigh with cheese on the

bottom of each bun. Lay some slices of chile pepper and 2 slices of bacon on each sandwich, and top with a piece of lettuce and 2 slices of tomato. Place one nicely browned onion ring on top and drizzle with a little more BBQ sauce. Top each sandwich with bun, and use a skewer to hold these behemoths together.

URGE GASTROPUB'S SCULPIN MAC & CHEESE

MARC LIAUTARD, CHEF, URGE GASTROPUB

[serves 4-6]

1 pound macaroni
1½ cups heavy cream
3 to 5 ounces half-and-half
¼ tablespoon ground nutmeg
½ bay leaf
½ tablespoon granulated garlic
   or garlic powder
½ teaspoon kosher salt,
   or to taste

¼ teaspoon ground black
   pepper, or to taste
6 ounces aged cheddar,
   shredded
3 ounces Ewephoria Gouda,
   shredded
3 to 6 ounces Sculpin IPA,
   as needed

[PREPARATION]

1. Bring a large pot of water to a boil. Cook pasta to desired doneness, according to directions on the package. Drain and set aside.

2. In a medium saucepan on medium heat, mix cream and half-and-half with nutmeg, bay leaf, granulated garlic, salt, and pepper, and bring to a boil.

3. Reduce heat to low and add the cheeses. Once cheeses have melted completely, remove from heat and add beer to taste.

4. Combine the pasta and cheese sauce, mixing well to coat thoroughly. Season with salt and pepper to taste and pour into a serving dish.

"Being an American gastropub, we try to focus on the great bar classics," says Grant Tondro (above, right), owner and founder of Urge. "So, when we were developing new things for the menu, Chef Marc (above, left) came up with these mac-and-cheese bites, which were small bits of deep-fried mac-and-cheese with a really awesome cheese sauce." Grant explains that Sculpin was the perfect beer to use for this dish, because "its bitterness is subtle but not overpowering." The cheese sauce for the bites eventually grew into the cheese sauce for this mac-and-cheese special, which is what you see here.

Grant says that an IPA works perfectly in this dish (and as a paring for it) because the hoppy bitterness plays off the rich fattiness of the cheese. "You don't want to eat a lot of bitter food," Grant explains, "but you want it to be a layer of flavor in some things."

PERFECT PAIRING

SPICY CURRY WITH CRISPY PORK BELLY AND HOP OIL

NEVA PARKER, HEAD OF LABORATORY OPERATIONS, WHITE LABS   [serves 6-8]

"Growing up, my grandmother Phon Kim used to make curry a lot from scratch," recalls Neva Parker, *"and so for this recipe, which is my grandmother's curry, I do it from scratch." The rest of the ingredients, Neva says, were her additions— they're ingredients she thinks go especially well with the red curry. She wanted to incorporate an IPA into the dish, but she found that cooking with it in this recipe didn't quite work. So she came up with the hop oil idea: "It adds just a touch of that hop without having to cook it."*

Chef's Note: *Start this recipe at least 24 hours in advance. Hop pellets and hop flowers are available at home brew supply stores.*

For the marinade:
24 ounces (two 12-ounce bottles) malty brown ale, divided use
1 tablespoon crushed white peppercorns
3 Kaffir lime leaves, shredded
Kosher salt
1 pound whole boneless pork belly, skin scored crosswise
2 tablespoons palm sugar or brown sugar

For the hop oil:
¼ ounce Cascade, Centennial, or Simcoe hop pellets, or ½ ounce whole hop flowers
½ cup extra-virgin olive oil

For the red curry paste:
4 dried chiles, seeded and soaked in warm water

1 stalk lemongrass, outer ribs removed, thinly sliced
4 cloves garlic
2 shallots, sliced
1 (2-inch piece) of galangal root, peeled and chopped
1 teaspoon Kaffir lime zest, or 2 to 3 Kaffir lime leaves, shredded
1 teaspoon shrimp paste (available at Asian markets)

For the curry:
2 tablespoons red curry paste (see recipe or use pre-made paste. I prefer Mae Ploy brand, sold at Asian markets)
1 tablespoon canola oil or vegetable oil
1 (14-ounce) can thick coconut milk
4 cups chicken stock or vegetable stock   **continued >**

PERFECT PAIRING

Prevailing wisdom has it that spicy dishes pair exceedingly well with IPAs, so why break tradition? You could also go with a pale ale, but a racier, hoppier, more full-bodied beer will play off the spice, the fat, and the citrus notes in this dish. Great IPAs? The list seems endless: **PORT BREWING'S MONGO, BALLAST POINT'S SCULPIN, GREEN FLASH'S WEST COAST IPA, STONE'S RUINATION...**

4 Kaffir lime leaves
1 teaspoon fish sauce, or to taste
1 small butternut squash, cut into ½-inch cubes
1 red bell pepper, julienned
Salt and freshly ground black pepper, to taste
Crushed red pepper, to taste
1 Kaffir lime, zested, or 2 Kaffir lime leaves, finely shredded

Finishing touches:
Jasmine rice

[PREPARATION]

1. Make the marinade: Combine 12 ounces (1 bottle) of the beer with the crushed white peppercorns, shredded lime leaves, and salt in a shallow pan and marinate pork belly overnight, turning often. Remove from refrigerator 1 hour before cooking.

2. Make the hop oil: Combine the hops and olive oil and let steep overnight. Strain solids from oil.

3. If making curry paste: Combine all ingredients and blend to a paste, using a food processor.

4. Make the curry: Heat oil on medium-high heat in a large pot, and add curry paste. Break up the paste into the oil and stir frequently until fragrant but not burning. Add the coconut milk and reduce heat to medium. Cook until the oil separates from the coconut milk, about 10 to 15 minutes.

5. In a small saucepan, combine the remaining beer, palm sugar, and a pinch of salt to make a glaze for the pork belly. Cook on medium heat until reduced by half, about 20 minutes.

6. Meanwhile, add the stock, Kaffir lime leaves, and fish sauce to coconut mixture, and simmer.

7. Preheat a broiler.

8. Remove pork belly from marinade and pat dry. Sprinkle salt and pepper on both sides, and brush the glaze onto the skin side.

9. Broil the pork belly until it is cooked through and the

skin is deep brown and is crispy, about 20 minutes. Remove from oven and let rest.

10. Add the butternut squash to the curry, increasing heat to medium, and cook until the squash is tender but not mushy, about 7 minutes. Add bell pepper and cook another 2 minutes. Add salt, pepper, and crushed red pepper to taste.

11. Cut the pork belly into 2-inch cubes. Ladle curry into a wide bowl and nestle the pork belly into the curry. Drizzle with a bit of hop oil and top with zest of Kaffir lime or shredded Kaffir lime leaf. Serve with a scoop of jasmine rice, if desired.

SEARSUCKER'S CALI BELGIQUE SHORT RIB SANDWICH
WITH HORSERADISH SAUCE

SHANE MCINTYRE, EXECUTIVE CHEF, SEARSUCKER   *[serves 4–6]*

Executive Chef Shane McIntyre explains that, "at Searsucker, when we make this recipe, we use about a gallon of Stone Cali Belgique in with the stocks for the braise. Now that's cooking with beer!" Of course, when preparing this at home, you'll only need 24 ounces to get that great beer kick in the sauce. The trick, when using a beer with this much hops, is not to let it boil, because that brings out the bitterness. That's why a low and slow braise at 300°F is the perfect way to go.

For the short ribs:
2 tablespoons canola oil or vegetable oil
2 pounds boneless short ribs
4 ribs celery, cut in small dice
2 yellow onions, cut in small dice
3 carrots, cut in small dice
4 cloves garlic
24 ounces Stone Cali Belgique (or other Belgian-inspired strong ale)
3 cups beef stock
3 cups chicken stock
2 sprigs thyme
1 tablespoon black peppercorns
2 bay leaves

For the horseradish sauce:
1 cup sour cream
1 tablespoon Worcestershire sauce
1 tablespoon Atomic Horseradish Sauce or other hot horseradish sauce
Salt and freshly ground black pepper, to taste

Finishing touches:
French rolls
Crispy fried onions
Pesto
Handful of fresh arugula

[PREPARATION]
1. Preheat oven to 300°F.
2. Prepare the short ribs: In a medium sauté pan, heat the oil to near smoking and sear the short ribs on both sides until golden brown. Remove

continued >

PERFECT PAIRING

"There's a lot of yeasty, malty flavor in **STONE'S CALI BELGIQUE**," Shane explains, "but also a good amount of hop, which pairs so, so well with the fattiness of the short rib."

from pan and set aside.

3. In the same pan, sauté the celery, onion, carrots, and garlic until caramelized (about 10 minutes).

4. Place the short ribs and vegetable mix into an ovenproof roasting pan and cover with the beer, beef stock, and chicken stock. Add the thyme, peppercorns, and bay leaves, cover with foil, and cook in the oven for 3½ hours, or until fork-tender and the meat pulls away easily when touched. Remove from the oven and let cool in the braising liquid. (Once the short ribs are cool, you can portion out the meat, or you can strain the braising liquid and refrigerate the short ribs overnight in the liquid, which will enhance the final flavor. You can reheat the meat in a hot sauté pan before serving.)

5. Make the horseradish sauce: In a small bowl, mix all the ingredients together and refrigerate until needed.

6. Assemble the sandwiches: At Searsucker, short rib sandwiches are served for lunch, and here's how they "roll:" Take a French roll (the softest you can find) and fill it with about 1 cup of shredded short ribs. Add some crispy fried onions and some pesto, if desired. Sauce it with 1 tablespoon of horseradish sauce and top it with fresh arugula for crunch.

CINNAMON-DUSTED PORK TENDERLOIN
WITH JALAPEÑO-YAM HASH, CILANTRO PESTO AND CHOCOLATE STOUT MOLE

BRANDON HERNÁNDEZ, AWARD-WINNING FOOD-AND-BEER JOURNALIST   *[serves 4]*

"Being a native San Diegan, I've grown up on — and adore — Mexican cuisine," says Brandon. "To me, nothing is more iconic than the ingredients and flavors of a great mole." Although Brandon loves the luscious black mole of Oaxaca, which gets its intensity from small, late additions of Mexican chocolate, his recipe gets its cocoa tinge from a large early pour of chocolate stout, which reduces along with chiles, nuts, and dried fruits.

For the spice blend:
¼ cup salt
2 tablespoons ground cumin
2 tablespoons garlic powder
2 tablespoons onion powder
2 tablespoons smoked paprika
1 tablespoon ground cinnamon
1 tablespoon chili powder
1 tablespoon ground dried oregano
1 tablespoon freshly ground black
  pepper
¾ teaspoon ground allspice

For the pesto:
1¼ cups cilantro, chopped
2 tablespoons cotija cheese,
  crumbled
2 tablespoons almonds
1 clove garlic
Grapeseed oil
Salt and freshly ground black
  pepper, to taste

For the mole:
6 tablespoons olive oil
6 corn tortillas
3 ancho chiles, stemmed and
  seeded
3 New Mexico chiles, stemmed
  and seeded
2 pasilla chiles, stemmed and
  seeded
¾ cup red onion, chopped
3 tablespoons garlic, minced
¾ cup almonds
3 cups chicken stock
2 cups Young's Double Chocolate
  Stout
6 Roma tomatoes, peeled, seeded,
  and chopped
¾ teaspoon ground cinnamon
¼ teaspoon ground cloves
6 tablespoons raisins
2 tablespoons pure maple syrup
2 tablespoons honey   **continued >**

PERFECT PAIRING

"It would seem a dish built on chocolate stout would pair best with that beer," Brandon explains. "But no one ingredient defines mole. It is a melding of many diverse ingredients that come together to create a unique, multi-layered flavor." Brandon says the dried fruit, caramel, nutmeg, and subtler chocolate notes of abbey dubbels, specifically **THE LOST ABBEY'S LOST AND FOUND ALE**, pair exceptionally well with this dish.

1 tablespoon lime juice
Salt and freshly ground black pepper, to taste

For the hash:
1 tablespoon bourbon whiskey
2 tablespoons currants
1 large garnet yam
2 teaspoons unsalted butter
¼ cup yellow onion, finely diced
3 tablespoons jalapeño
   pepper, seeded and
   finely diced*
Salt and freshly ground
   black pepper, to
   taste
½ tablespoon garlic,
   finely chopped
Olive oil

For the pork tenderloin:
3 tablespoons olive oil
2 pork tenderloins, trimmed

[PREPARATION]
1. Make the spice blend: Combine all of the ingredients until completely incorporated. Set aside or store in an airtight container.
2. Make the pesto: Place the cilantro, cheese, almonds, and garlic in the bowl of a food processor. Turn on the machine and slowly pour in the oil until the pesto reaches a spreadable but not runny consistency. Season with salt and pepper to taste and set aside.
3. Make the mole: Heat the oil in a large skillet over high heat. Fry the tortillas, one at a time, until crispy, 20 to 30 seconds per side. Remove, drain on paper towels, and transfer to the bowl of a food processor.
4. Reduce heat to medium-high. Add the chiles to the skillet and cook until crisp, about 20 seconds per side.

Remove and transfer to food processor. Add the onion and garlic to the skillet and cook, stirring occasionally, for 2 minutes. Remove and transfer to food processor.
5. Reduce heat to medium. Remove all but 3 table-spoons of the oil from the skillet or add more oil, if needed. Add the almonds, toast until golden brown, 2 to 3 minutes, and transfer to food processor.
6. Add 1½ cups of the stock to the food processor and purée the mixture. Pour the purée into a large saucepan over medium-high heat. Add the stout, tomatoes, cinnamon, cloves, raisins, and remaining stock, and bring to a boil. Reduce the heat to medium and simmer, stirring occasionally, until the mixture thickens to a sauce consistency.
7. Transfer the mixture to a food processor. Add the maple syrup, honey, and lime juice, and purée. Pour the purée back into the saucepan and simmer for 10 minutes. Season with salt and pepper to taste and keep warm, or store, refrigerated, in an airtight container, for up to 10 days.
8. Heat oven to 400°F.
9. Make the hash: Bring the whiskey to a boil in a small saucepan. Remove from heat and pour into a small bowl containing the currants. Let stand for 20 minutes and drain off any excess liquid. Set the currants aside.
10. Use a fork to poke holes in the yam. Place it on a baking sheet lined with parchment paper. Place in the oven and bake until tender, about 30 minutes. Remove from oven and let cool. Peel the yam, mash and set aside.

continued >

CINNAMON-DUSTED PORK TENDERLOIN
continued from page 119

11. Heat the butter in a large sauté pan over medium heat. Add the onion, jalapeño, and currants. Season with salt and pepper, and cook until the vegetables are soft and tender, about 6 minutes. Add the mashed yam and garlic, and cook, stirring occasionally, for 5 minutes. Remove from heat and transfer to a shallow baking dish. Smooth the mixture into an even layer. When cool enough to handle, use a 3-inch ring mold to form 1-inch thick patties. Heat a thin layer of olive oil in a large skillet over medium-high heat and sauté the patties until golden brown, about 1 minute per side. Remove from heat and keep warm.

12. Prepare the pork: Heat the oil in a large sauté pan over high heat. Rub the tenderloins evenly with the spice blend and place the tenderloins in the skillet (keeping them straight). Cook until browned, about 45 seconds on each side. Remove from the skillet and transfer to a baking sheet. Transfer to the oven and bake to medium doneness, about 10 minutes. Transfer tenderloins to a plate and cover with aluminum foil. Let stand for 10 minutes.

13. To serve, ladle some of the mole into the middle of a round plate so that it forms a circle. Cut the tenderloins into ½-inch-thick slices. Place a hash patty in the center of the plate and arrange slices of pork around the patty. Spoon a small mound of the pesto atop the patty and serve immediately.

Note: Wear gloves when chopping peppers, and avoid touching your eyes.

TEMPEH SHEPHERD'S PIE
WITH STONE IPA GARLICKY MASHED POTATOES

RECIPE BY ALEX CARBALLO, CHIEF CULINARY PHILOSOPHER,
STONE BREWING WORLD BISTRO & GARDENS

[serves 8]

Chef's Note: *Brewer's yeast is available at most grocery stores and natural food stores.*

For the roasted garlic:
1 head garlic
1 tablespoon extra-virgin
  olive oil
Salt and freshly ground
  black pepper, to taste

For the potatoes:
2 pounds Yukon gold
  potatoes, quartered
2 tablespoons garlic-
  infused oil
¼ cup Stone IPA, or more
  as needed
¼ teaspoon brewer's yeast
1 teaspoon fresh parsley,
  chopped

For the filling:
2 pounds tempeh
1 tablespoon ground
  pasilla chiles
1 tablespoon ground
  chipotle chiles
1 tablespoon garlic powder
2 teaspoons ground cumin
2 teaspoons salt
4 tablespoons olive oil
½ cup sweet onions, diced
½ cup carrot, diced
½ cup celery, diced
½ zucchini, diced
3 cloves garlic, minced
¼ cup dry white wine
2 cups shredded cheddar
  cheese   **continued >**

Greg Koch, CEO & co-founder of Stone Brewing Co., often likes to eat vegetarian, so he's ensured that in addition to a menu that utilizes fresh, organic, local produce, there are always vegetarian and vegan options available at Stone Brewing World Bistro & Gardens.

PERFECT PAIRING

Stone's official beer-and-food pairing expert, "Dr." Bill Sysak, recommends **STONE SMOKED PORTER** or a delicious brown ale with this recipe. "This is a soul-satisfying dish that pairs beautifully with brown ales and porters," he says. And Greg? He says, "I'll have an IPA, thank you very much."

[PREPARATION]

1. Roast the garlic: Preheat oven to 350°F. Cut the top ¼ inch off the garlic, leaving the head intact but exposing the individual cloves. Place the garlic, cut side up, on a large sheet of foil and drizzle with oil and season with salt and pepper. Gather the foil up around the garlic, twist the top to seal, and place in the oven for 1 hour. Let the garlic cool completely before gently squeezing the cloves out.

2. Make the potatoes: In a medium saucepan on high heat, cover the potatoes with cold salted water and bring to a boil. Lower the heat to medium, cover, and cook until the potatoes are tender and easily pierced with a fork (about 15 to 20 minutes.).

3. Drain the potatoes, place them into a medium bowl, and add the roasted garlic, beer, brewer's yeast, and parsley. Use a potato masher or ricer to work the potatoes to the desired consistency. (If they are too stiff, add more beer.) Season with salt and pepper to taste.

4. Make the filling: In a large bowl, crumble the tempeh with your hands and add the chile powders, garlic powder, cumin, and salt. Stir until thoroughly combined.

5. Heat 2 tablespoons of olive oil in a large saucepan or cast-iron skillet over medium-high heat until the oil begins to shimmer. Add the onion, carrot, and celery, and sauté until they begin to soften, about 3 minutes. Add the zucchini and cook an additional 2 minutes. Stir in the garlic and cook for 1 more minute.

6. Deglaze the pan with the white wine, stirring, scraping up, and dissolving any brown bits that may be sticking to the pan. Once the white wine is mostly evaporated, move the vegetables to the outer edges of the pan, making a well in the center. Add the remaining 2 tablespoons of olive oil and heat slightly.

7. Add the tempeh to the well, stirring to coat. Stir everything together, sautéing until the tempeh is heated through and the vegetables are tender, about 4 to 5 minutes.

Greg Koch: "I love this recipe because many people don't know what tempeh is. They order it, eat it, love it, and never know they've eaten a vegetarian dish. It's that good."

8. Preheat the broiler.

9. Pour the tempeh mixture into a 9-by-13-inch baking pan and spread into an even layer. Top with an even layer of the mashed potatoes and sprinkle the top with cheese.

10. Broil until the cheese is melted, bubbly, and golden brown, about 5 to 7 minutes.

This recipe was used with permission. Originally published in "The Craft of Stone Brewing Co." © 2011 by Ten Speed Press, Berkeley, California.

THREE-DAY MISSION AMBER PORK BELLY (AKA "BEER BELLY")

KARL PROHASKA, EXECUTIVE CHEF, HANDLERY HOTEL SAN DIEGO   *[serves 6-8]*

In addition to being the executive chef at the Handlery, Karl Prohaska is a KCBS Barbeque Competitor — the man knows pork. Over time, he has developed techniques, like curing and weighting, which greatly enhance his pork belly recipes. "A lot of the pork bellies I've had over the years were delicious, but they lacked a certain flavor from the braising liquid not being drawn into them," Karl explains, "That's I why I started curing them first. This dries them out a bit so they suck in the braising liquid and all that beer flavor when they cook."

Chef's Note: *This recipe is best started 3 days ahead. It's still very good if you skip Day 1 and Day 3, but it's great if you're able to follow all of the instructions.*

For the pork and cure:
5 pounds whole pork belly
¾ cup molasses
2 pounds brown sugar
1 pound kosher salt
3 tablespoons herbes d'Provence

For the braise:
All-purpose flour seasoned with salt and black pepper, as needed
3 shallots, sliced
1 medium onion, diced

6 celery stalks, sliced
3 carrots, sliced
2 tablespoons garlic, chopped
22 ounces Mission Amber beer
1 pound canned San Marzano tomatoes
Chicken stock, as needed
2 tablespoons unsalted butter
Olive oil

Finishing touch:
Tomato-mint jam

[PREPARATION]

1. Prepare the pork: Rub the entire pork belly with molasses. Combine the brown sugar, salt, and herbs, and pack the mixture on all sides of the pork belly. Cover and refrigerate for 24 hours.

2. Preheat oven to 300°F.

3. Wash off the cure and pat the pork belly dry. Coat the pork lightly in seasoned flour. Heat a large, oven-safe pot or Dutch oven over high heat and

continued >

PERFECT PAIRING

Chef Prohaska loves serving this dish with **MISSION'S AMBER**, "because I think they make a great one." A nicely balanced amber will have the maltiness to enhance the sweetness of the sauce and pork, but will also have some refreshing hoppy bitterness to cut through the fat and sugar.

sear the pork on all sides. Transfer pork to a plate.

4. Add shallots, onion, celery, and carrots to the pan and cook for 5 minutes. Add garlic and cook for 2 minutes. Deglaze the pan with beer, scraping the bottom to loosen and dissolve the brown solids (fond). Add tomatoes with their liquid and bring mixture to a simmer.

5. Add the seared pork belly to the liquid. (Add additional chicken stock if needed so meat is submerged.) Cover with a piece of parchment paper or foil cut to the size of the pot and then cover with a lid. Place in the oven and braise for 2½ hours. To test, insert a skewer into the meat (it should slide in easily).

6. Remove the pan from the oven and carefully lift the pork from the pan. Allow it to cool for 30 minutes before putting it in a storage container that allows it to sit flat.

Cover the meat with plastic wrap and weight it before placing it in the refrigerator to cool entirely — overnight is best. (The weighting allows the meat to compact during the cooling process.)

7. Strain the vegetables from the braising liquid and refrigerate.

8. Skim any collected fat from the top of the braising liquid, pour into a medium saucepan, and reduce by half, or until the liquid becomes dark and rich. Once the liquid is reduced, taste it to check seasoning. Swirl in 2 tablespoons of unsalted butter and keep the liquid warm.

9. Cut the pork into servings about 3 inches square. Heat olive oil in a skillet and sear the squares until they are heated through. Top each serving with sauce and tomato jam, and serve immediately.

EASY AZTEC BEER MAC & CHEEZE

CLAUDIA FAULK, CO-FOUNDER AND PARTNER, AZTEC BREWING COMPANY   *[serves 4–6]*

Claudia Faulk (with husband John and son Tristan) says she has eaten a lot of mac 'n'cheese in her time, and, in her experience, it "never has a lot of flavor." So she set out to create one that does. Being quasi-vegetarian, as she puts it, she also wanted to create a dish that was vegetarian but that still excited her palate. That's where the paprika and the blend of boldly flavored cheeses comes in.

For the mac & cheeze

1 pound penne rigate pasta (I like Ronzoni Garden Delight)
3 tablespoons butter
¼ cup all-purpose flour
1½ cups milk
1½ cups Aztec Amber beer
8 ounces cheddar cheese, freshly grated
4 ounces Monterey Jack cheese, freshly grated
6 ounces Parmesan cheese, freshly grated
½ teaspoon smoked paprika
1 pinch black pepper
½ cup Italian-style panko bread crumbs

Finishing touches:

Extra grated cheese and a sprinkle of garlic powder
Crispy bacon, optional

[PREPARATION]

1. Boil water and cook the pasta according to the package directions, but decrease the cooking time by 1 to 2 minutes. (The pasta will finish cooking in the oven.)

2. Preheat oven to 375°F. Heat a saucepan over medium heat and add the butter. When the butter is melted and sizzling, whisk in the flour to create a roux. Cook until bubbly and golden in color, about 2 minutes.

3. Add the milk and beer to the saucepan, whisking constantly. Add the cheeses and stir until melted. Turn the heat to low and continue to stir, cooking for 5 to 6 minutes while the mixture thickens. (It won't get as thick as regular mac and cheese because of the beer, but you want it to thicken a little bit.) Stir in the pepper and paprika.

continued >

PERFECT PAIRING

AZTEC'S AMBER is a malty, medium-bodied ale with a firm backbone of hoppiness that, as Claudia says, adds a "nice, zippy component" to the dish. Recommended pairing: Aztec Amber, or any malt-forward beer with enough hoppiness to balance, such as **PORT BREWING'S SHARK ATTACK** or **GREEN FLASH'S HOP HEAD RED.**

4. Put the pasta in a casserole dish. (Use a larger pan and spread the pasta out more if you like it crispy.) Pour the cheese sauce over the noodles, mixing gently to combine. You can add a little extra grated cheese, about ¾ cup, if you like.

5. Top with the bread crumbs and sprinkle with additional Parmesan cheese and a little garlic powder, if desired. Meat-lovers can add crispy bacon here, too! Bake for 25 to 30 minutes, until bubbly and golden on top.

6. Remove from the oven and cool for 5 minutes before serving. Delicious with a crisp green salad and a tall glass of great beer!

STOUT-BRAISED PORK BELLY
WITH COCOA CRUST AND RED BEET SLAW

MATT GORDON, OWNER AND FOUNDER, URBAN SOLACE RESTAURANT   *[serves 8]*

Chef's Note: *Start 4 days in advance of when you want to serve this dish. (It sounds hard, but it's really easy!) These are the 4 basic steps: 1. Cure the pork belly. 2. Braise the pork belly. 3. Cool the pork belly overnight. 4. Cut pork belly into portions, roast, and serve.*

For the cure:
½ cup granulated sugar
½ cup brown sugar
½ cup kosher salt
1 tablespoon ground cinnamon
1 teaspoon ground ginger
1 teaspoon ground allspice
1 tablespoon ground star anise
1 teaspoon ground cloves
1 teaspoon red chile flakes
2 tablespoons ground coriander
1 high-quality natural skinless pork belly, approximately 4 pounds (like Niman Ranch)

For the braising liquid:
½ cup garlic cloves, whole

3 stalks celery
1 yellow onion, coarsely chopped
24 ounces stout beer (we love Ballast Point and Coronado's coffee stouts for this)
3 quarts water

For the slaw:
1 to 2 large red beets, peeled and cut into strips
1 ear white sweet corn, grilled or roasted to caramelize the outside
¼ cup arugula leaves, cut in thin strips
¼ cup scallions, white part only, finely sliced
Pinch of salt and black pepper

continued >

Urban Solace is one of San Diego's best-loved casual, hip, and very cool places to sit and enjoy great-tasting food. Smack in the heart of North Park (the city's beer bar epicenter), the restaurant is frequently involved in celebrating San Diego beer. "We came up with this dish for a local beer event a few years ago," Matt Gordon remembers. "We were partnered with a local brewery that made great stout, so I created a recipe around that. It turned out so well that it has been on and off our menu ever since."

PERFECT PAIRING

This is a recipe that's designed with — and to go with — stout, so why fight it? Pair this hearty, satisfying, flavorful dish with a great stout (either with coffee notes or without). Coronado, Ballast Point, AleSmith, and Green Flash all make great stouts.

Matt Gordon: "This dish has evolved over time. Once we added the cocoa rub with the chile flakes and lime zest, it really pulled the whole thing together."

STOUT-BRAISED PORK BELLY
continued from page 129

For the slaw dressing:
1 teaspoon coriander seed, toasted
1 teaspoon red chile flakes
½ cup lime juice
½ cup orange juice
1 tablespoon grated lime zest
1 tablespoon granulated sugar
2 tablespoons olive oil
2 teaspoons kosher salt

For the cocoa spice rub:
2 tablespoons Valrhona cocoa powder
1 teaspoon ground fennel seed
1 teaspoon coriander seed
1 teaspoon red chile flakes
1 teaspoon grated lime zest

Finishing touches:
Thick-cut french fries, optional
Your favorite chimichurri, optional

[PREPARATION]
DAY 4
1. Make the cure: In a medium bowl, combine all the ingredients well. Completely coat the pork with the cure mixture, top and bottom, and place the pork in a baking dish. Coat with any remaining cure mixture. Cover tightly and refrigerate for 3 days.

DAY 2
2. Preheat oven to 350°F.
3. Braise the pork belly: You will need a baking dish large enough to accommodate the pork belly submerged in liquid. Scrape excess salt and spices off of cured belly (do not rinse). Place in the baking dish and add the garlic, celery, onion, beer, and water. Cover tightly with foil. Bake for 3½ to 4 hours, or until the pork is so tender it falls apart if you push at it with tongs.
4. Remove the meat from the oven and remove foil. Let cool in liquid for about 2 hours. Gently remove the meat from the liquid, reserving the liquid in the refrigerator, and place the pork on a baking sheet. Chill, covered, overnight.

DAY 1
5. Make the slaw and dressing: In a large bowl, combine all the slaw ingredients. Grind the coriander and the chile flakes in a spice grinder. Combine with all the remaining dressing ingredients and whisk or shake vigorously to incorporate. Mix slaw with dressing to coat well.
6. Preheat oven to 350°F.
7. Portion the belly: Cut the pork into roughly 3-inch squares. Combine the cocoa spice rub ingredients in a small bowl. Coat the meat side of the pork with the rub.
8. Sear the meat portions: In a hot sauté pan or on a griddle with a little olive oil, sear the spice-crusted side of the pork. Flip over pork pieces and place on a baking sheet in the oven until the pork is heated through and browning, about 12 minutes.
9. Serve the pork with red beet slaw, and, if desired, fries and a dollop of chimichurri. Also, If desired, heat the reserved braising liquid in a saucepan and boil until reduced to taste. Serve as a sauce with the pork.

SPICY IPA BURGER
WITH IPA ONION STRINGS AND APRICOT HABANERO KETCHUP

A.G. WARFIELD, EXECUTIVE CHEF, CHURCHILL'S PUB & GRILLE   *[serves 4]*

For the ketchup:
2 tablespoons butter
½ cup white onion, diced
2 fresh habanero peppers, diced*
6 fresh tomatoes, peeled and
  seeded
6 fresh apricots, pitted and diced
½ cup apple cider vinegar
½ cup water
2 cups tomato purée
½ cup brown sugar

For the burger patties:
1 tablespoon butter
1 cup onion, diced
½ cup red bell pepper, diced
8 ounces IPA (I like Alpine's Nelson)
1½ pounds ground chuck (80
  percent lean)
½ pound ground lamb

2 eggs, beaten
½ cup panko bread crumbs
4 jalapeño peppers, fire roasted and
  diced*
Salt and pepper

For the onion strings:
2 medium white onions, sliced
  paper-thin
8 ounces IPA (I like Port's High Tide)
3 cups vegetable oil
2 cups all-purpose flour
1 teaspoon salt
1 teaspoon pepper
1 teaspoon cayenne pepper

Finishing touches:
4 slices pepper Jack cheese
4 buns, such as artisan brioche
  buns or potato buns

continued >

San Diego is not only known as America's craft beer capital, it also has become the world's IPA capital. Churchill's is located only minutes from Stone, Port Brewing, Mother Earth, and Aztec, to name a few, so it makes a good deal of sense for Chef A.G. Warfield to have an IPA classic like this burger on his menu.

A.G.'s top choice is to pair this burger with **ALPINE'S NELSON**, but any great IPA will work. **PORT BREWING'S HIGH TIDE, MISSION'S SHIPWRECKED, CORONADO'S IDIOT, GREEN FLASH'S IMPERIAL**, and any great **STONE IPA** are other top choices.

PERFECT PAIRING

SPICY IPA BURGER WITH IPA ONION STRINGS

continued from page 131

[PREPARATION]

1. Make the ketchup: Heat the butter in a saucepan and sauté the onion and habanero until onion is translucent, about 3 to 5 minutes. Add the fresh tomato, apricot, apple cider vinegar, and water. Bring to a boil, reduce heat, and simmer for 15 minutes.

2. Add the tomato purée and brown sugar, and continue to simmer for 20 minutes. Pour the mixture into a food processor or blender and purée until smooth. Remove from food processor and cool to room temperature.

3. Make the burger patties: Heat the butter in a saucepan and sauté the diced onion and red bell pepper until the onion is translucent, about 3 to 5 minutes. Soak the peppers and onions in your favorite IPA for 1 hour.

4. Soak the onions for the strings: Put the sliced onion in a bowl and pour the IPA over it. Allow to soak for 1 hour.

5. Mix the ground chuck and ground lamb with the beer-soaked red-pepper-and-onion mixture. Add the beaten eggs, panko, and diced fire-roasted jalapeño, and incorporate well. Form the mixture into 8-ounce patties and refrigerate for at least 30 minutes.

6. Prepare and heat a grill on high.

7. Make the onion strings: In a small saucepan, heat oil to 325°F. In a bowl, mix flour, salt, pepper, and cayenne. Drain the soaked onions to remove any excess liquid. Toss onions in the seasoned flour and fry them in small batches. (If you fry too many at once, they will clump up.) Fry each batch for 2 to 3 minutes, or until crispy. Remove and drain on paper towels.

8. Grill the burgers: Salt and pepper the patties and cook on the grill to your liking. When you flip each burger, top with a slice of pepper Jack cheese, if desired.

9. To serve, slather each bun with habanero ketchup and place each burger on a bun. Top with a generous amount of IPA onion strings, pour a cold beer, and enjoy!

Note: Wear gloves when chopping peppers, and avoid touching your eyes.

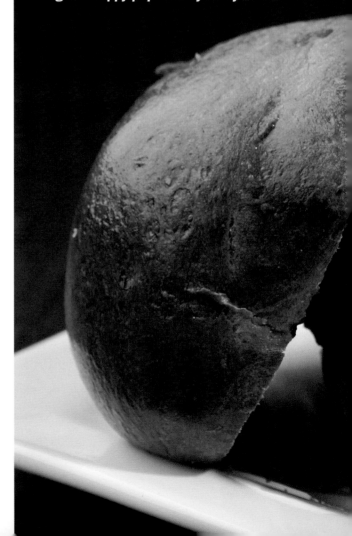

A.G. Warfield: "I originally created this dish for a pub regular who loved Alpine — especially Nelson IPA. That beer has wonderful notes of apricot, so I wanted to echo that in the ketchup. IPAs are perfect matches for spicy foods, and marinating the onions in the beer gives them that great hoppy pop when you fry them."

STONE SMOKED PORTER CHILI

MITCH STEELE, BREWMASTER, STONE BREWING CO.

[serves 10]

How did Mitch Steele know he was destined one day to become brewmaster at Stone Brewing Co.? Well, it might have been the fact that, even when he was brewer elsewhere, he had always used Stone Smoked Porter in this recipe. "It has always been the perfect beer to use in this dish," Mitch says. "It adds special layers of malty flavor along with some smoke and hoppiness." This chili is a Steele Family classic — Mitch has won several Super Bowl cookoffs with it, and he often prepares it for special family occasions.

Chef's Note: *This recipe is best with more than 48 hours of prep time: 24 hours for marinating and then 8 to 12 hours for smoking.*

For the marinade:
1 (4- to 5-pound) Boston butt
  or pork shoulder
2 cups Stone Smoked Porter
1 cup soy sauce
1 cup apple juice

For the rub:
1 cup brown sugar
⅔ cup smoked paprika
1 tablespoon garlic powder
1 tablespoon cumin
2 teaspoons mustard powder
1 teaspoon pepper
1 teaspoon salt
½ teaspoon ground cinnamon
Applewood chips, for smoking

For the basting spray:
1 cup Stone Smoked Porter
1 cup apple juice

For the chili:
1 tablespoon olive oil
1 onion, diced
1 (16-ounce) can tomato sauce
1 (10-ounce) can tomato purée
1 (22-ounce) bottle Stone Smoked Porter
  (save 8 ounces for drinking!)
Fresh chiles and ground dried chiles, to taste
  (I like a blend of medium and hot chiles,
  but always include chipotle pepper)
1 green bell pepper, chopped
2 tablespoons cumin
1 tablespoon chili powder
1 teaspoon red pepper flakes
1 teaspoon garlic powder
½ teaspoon freshly ground black pepper
Salt, to taste
½ teaspoon ground cinnamon
1 small can tomato paste
Hot sauce (Tapatio or Sriracha), to taste
1 can kidney beans (optional)

continued >

PERFECT PAIRING

Here's a recipe you can either complement or contrast beautifully with beer. The obvious complement would be a smoked porter or some kind of chile porter. For contrast, a hoppy, crisp, refreshing beer — such as **STONE PALE ALE** or **IPA** — would cut through the rich, fatty, smoky flavors and offset some of the heat from the spices.

[PREPARATION]

1. Marinate the pork: In a large zipper-top bag, combine the pork with the beer, soy sauce, and apple juice. Refrigerate 24 hours.

2. Prepare the rub: The night before smoking the pork, combine all the rub ingredients in a bowl and mix well. Remove the pork from the marinade, pat dry with paper towels, and cover completely with the rub. Refrigerate overnight.

3. Smoke the pork: Preheat a grill or smoker to around 225°F. Add the applewood chips and smoke the pork for 8 to 12 hours.

4. Make the basting spray: Combine the beer and the apple juice. Baste the pork periodically with the spray while the pork is smoking.

5. The pork is done when it pulls apart easily. Remove from heat, cool, pull the meat from the bone, and chop into large pieces.

6. Assemble the chili: In a medium sauté pan on medium heat, heat the oil and sauté the onion until translucent. Add the tomato sauce and tomato purée, and stir together well.

7. In a crockpot, combine the onion and tomato mixture with the beer, green bell pepper, chiles, and spices, and heat on the low setting for several hours.

8. Two to 3 hours before serving the chili, add approximately 3 cups of the smoked pork to the crockpot, along with the tomato paste, hot sauce, and the beans, if desired.

9. Taste continually while cooking to evaluate proper levels of heat and flavor. When the chili is done, ladle it into bowls and serve.

BBQ'D JERKED BARLEYWINE CHICKEN WITH SUCCOTASH

BRANDON BROOKS, EXECUTIVE CHEF, SOL MARKETS

[serves 6]

"*Green Flash's barleywine is one of my favorite beers to cook with,*" *says Brandon Brooks, executive chef at SOL Markets.* "*It's got such great malty character, it's rich, and it adds some of the same acid and aromatic qualities to a dish that you get from white wine.*" *The actual active time required for this recipe is minimal, but — with a little do-ahead planning — you'll get results that are truly rewarding.*

Chef's Note: *The chicken is best when marinated overnight.*

For the chicken:
4 pounds chicken, preferably boneless thighs
1 shallot, finely diced
4 garlic cloves, finely diced
1 red onion, finely diced
4 to 5 habanero peppers, roasted and seeded*
6 limes, juiced
2 blood oranges, juiced
2 tablespoons salt
1 tablespoon pepper
1 tablespoon brown sugar
2 tablespoons honey
1 cinnamon stick
2 teaspoons allspice
1 teaspoon nutmeg
22 ounces (1 bottle) Green Flash Barleywine

For the succotash:
2 tablespoons olive oil
½ cup red onion, cut in small dice
½ cup celery, cut in small dice
½ cup carrot, cut in small dice
⅛ cup Anaheim peppers, cut in small dice
1 clove garlic, finely chopped
½ cup fresh shelling beans (or lima beans)
1 tablespoon butter
Salt and pepper, to taste

[PREPARATION]

1. Marinate the chicken: Combine all ingredients, including the chicken, in a large bowl. Marinate, refrigerated, for at least 2 hours but preferably overnight.

continued >

PERFECT PAIRING

GREEN FLASH BARLEYWINE is one of the best around. It has a big, malty character that stands up to cooking and even reducing. If you can get an extra bottle or two, this is a relatively affordable beer that also ages well. Other great barleywines include **STONE'S OLD GUARDIAN** and **ALESMITH'S OLD NUMBSKULL**.

Brandon Brooks:
"The best thing you can do for this recipe is allow the chicken to marinate as much as possible, up to 24 hours. That's how all the great flavors of the marinade get into the meat before grilling."

2. When the chicken is ready to cook, prepare the succotash. In a hot sauté pan combine the olive oil, onion, celery, carrot, Anaheim pepper, and garlic. Cook for 4 minutes, or until the onions and celery begin to soften. Stirring continuously, add the beans. Cook for another 4 minutes and remove from the heat. Stir in butter, salt and pepper, mix thoroughly, and set aside.

3. Lightly coat the cooking surface of a grill with olive oil before turning it on to medium heat. Allow the grill to heat up for 5 or 10 minutes before placing the marinated chicken on the grill.

4. Grill the chicken for 4 to 5 minutes on each side, until cooked through. Use a meat thermometer to ensure the chicken has reached an internal temperature of 165° to 170°F.

5. Assemble this dish on a large platter, family style, by placing the succotash in the center and arranging the chicken, hot from the grill, on top.

Note: Wear gloves when working with peppers, and avoid touching your eyes.

MISSION AMBER ALE BRAISED SHORT RIBS

TAMI RATLIFFE, OWNER, CAFÉ CHLOE

[serves 8-10]

Tami Ratliffe (center, with Mission Brewery owners Sarah and Dan Selis) explains that for a long time, the short ribs on her menu were made with the typical ingredients, like red wine and balsamic vinegar — but that was before "San Diego became the craft beer capital of the United States." Then her good friends Dan and Sarah Selis opened Mission Brewery just a few blocks away. "That's when I realized, oh, my gosh, let's use Mission beer!" Tami recalls. "And it worked beautifully!"

Chef's Note: *You can make your own demi-glace by making a beef or veal stock and boiling it until it is reduced by half. You can also buy great-quality demi-glace online or at the specialty food and cookware stores.*

¼ cup extra-virgin olive oil
5 pounds boneless beef short ribs, cut into 4-ounce portions
Kosher salt and freshly ground black pepper
4 carrots, peeled and cut into ¼-inch dice
3 medium yellow onions, cut into ½-inch dice
3 celery stalks, cut into ¼-inch dice

12 garlic cloves
4 ounces tomato paste
24 ounces Mission Amber Ale
4 cups veal demi-glace
1 bunch fresh thyme sprigs
1 bunch fresh rosemary sprigs
2 bay leaves

Finishing touches:
Sweet potato purée
Roasted brussels sprouts

[PREPARATION]

1. Preheat oven to 325°F. In a large, heavy-bottomed ovenproof skillet, heat half the olive oil over high heat until smoking. Season the short ribs aggressively with kosher salt and pepper, and place them 5 at a time in the hot oil. Sear until deep brown on all sides, about 10 minutes per batch. Heat the remaining oil as needed. Transfer the short ribs to a plate and set aside.

2. Add the carrots, onions, celery, and garlic to the skillet and cook over

continued >

PERFECT PAIRING

MISSION'S AMBER ALE is the perfect accompaniment to this recipe because it has enough hoppiness to cut through the rich meat but also enough maltiness to complement the dark sauce. Hop-forward red ales would also work well, as would pale ales or even pilsners, if you want to go light.

high heat until browned and softened, 6 to 7 minutes.

3. Season the vegetables with salt and pepper, and stir in the tomato paste. Cook for 5 minutes, being careful not to burn the tomato paste.

4. Add the beer. Scrape the bottom of the skillet with a wooden spoon to dislodge the brown bits and add the demi-glace. Wrap the thyme, rosemary, and bay leaf in cheesecloth and tie with kitchen twine. Add the sachet to the skillet and bring the mixture to a boil.

5. Return the short ribs to the skillet, cover, and cook in the oven for 2 hours.

6. Uncover the skillet and continue to cook for 30 minutes, or until the meat is fork-tender. Remove the short ribs from the braising liquid, strain, and return the strained liquid to the skillet. Use a ladle or a kitchen spoon to skim the fat from the braising liquid. Boil the liquid until it is reduced to sauce consistency and serve it with the short ribs along with roasted brussels sprouts and sweet potato purée.

COQ AU BIER

KYLE BERGMAN, CHEF, GRILL AT THE LODGE AT TORREY PINES *[serves 2]*

"This is the beer-lover's take on the classic French dish Coq au Vin or the classic Belgian braised chicken," Kyle explains. "Instead of the traditional red wine from the French version, I've substituted a brown ale and some balsamic vinegar. For the Belgian classic, they usually use a Belgian brown or a dubbel." The result is a wonderfully malty, rich, sauce that has the perfect balance of sweetness and acidity. Kyle's favorite beer for this recipe is New English Brewers Special Brown. "It's a great cooking beer," he explains. "It has just the right amount of malt and hop, and it's not overly bitter."

Chef's Note: *This recipe is best when started a day ahead.*

For the marinade:
2 quarts brown ale (I like New English Brewers Special Brown)
1 quart chicken stock
2 cups molasses
2 cups balsamic vinegar
1 carrot
1 celery rib
1 small onion
1 bouquet garni (5 sprigs fresh thyme, 3 sprigs fresh parsley, 2 bay leaves, and 10 whole black peppercorns tied securely in cheesecloth)
2 chicken thighs, skin removed
2 chicken breasts, skin on
Salt and freshly ground black pepper, to taste
Olive oil

For the vegetables:
2 shallots, peeled and halved
1 parsnip, peeled and cut in medium to large dice
1 carrot, peeled and cut in medium to large dice
1 turnip, peeled and cut in medium to large dice
1 celery root, peeled and cut in medium to large dice
Olive oil
½ tablespoon thyme leaves
1 bay leaf
Salt and freshly ground black pepper, to taste

Finishing touches:
Mashed potatoes
Crusty bread

continued >

PERFECT PAIRING

Chef Kyle says, "You could certainly drink a brown ale with this dish. The brown has a natural affinity because it's used in the recipe. But I'd prefer a Belgian dubbel or even a Blanc de Brussels. You don't want a big, heavy dish and a big, heavy beer. You kind of want one or the other."

[PREPARATION]

THE DAY BEFORE SERVING

1. Make the marinade for the chicken thighs:
Bring the ale, stock, molasses, vinegar, whole carrot, celery stalk, onion, and bouquet garni to a boil in a large pot and simmer for 20 minutes. Remove from the heat and let the mixture cool. Strain into a nonreactive dish. Add the chicken thighs and marinate, refrigerated, overnight.

THE DAY TO SERVE

2. Preheat oven to 350°F.

3. Prepare the vegetables: Place the shallots, parsnip, carrot, turnip, and celery root in a large bowl. Toss to coat with olive oil, thyme, and bay leaf. Season with salt and pepper and spread the vegetables on a baking sheet lined with parchment paper or foil. Place in the oven and roast for 30 to 40 minutes, stirring occasionally to brown evenly. Remove from oven and set aside.

4. Lower oven temperature to 300°F.

5. Remove the chicken thighs from the marinade and place them in a shallow braising pan. Cover the thighs halfway with the marinade, cover the pan, and place it in the oven. Braise for 1 hour, or until the thighs are cooked through. Add the roasted vegetables and the chicken breasts to the braising liquid to warm. Season to taste with salt and pepper.

6. Cook the chicken breasts: Increase oven to 350°F. Season the breasts with salt and pepper and a little olive oil and sear in a hot skillet before roasting in the oven until just done (20 to 30 minutes).

7. Serve immediately by placing one thigh, one breast, some vegetables in a shallow soup bowl. Cover with just enough braising liquid to coat well. Suggested accompaniments: mashed potatoes and crusty bread to soak up extra sauce.

QUAD-BRAISED OSSO BUCO

"DR." BILL SYSAK, CERTIFIED CICERONE & CRAFT BEER AMBASSADOR,
STONE BREWING CO.

[serves 4-6]

"Dr." Bill Sysak is not only a certified cicerone (the beer equivalent of a sommelier), he's also an accomplished chef. That's why, when anyone at Stone Brewing Co. wants to know what food goes well with what beer, Dr. Bill is the guy they ask. So what's the beer for this great dish? You guessed it — Belgian quad. "I don't usually pair the same beer with the one used in the recipe," Bill explains, "but drinking a great quad with this dish really elevates both the food and the beer in a special way."

Chef's Note: *Recipe adapted by Bill Sysak from an original recipe by Heather Lewis / Beer Bitty (beerbitty.com)*

3 pounds beef shanks
Salt and freshly ground black
   pepper
2 tablespoons all-purpose flour
½ cup pancetta (or bacon), diced
1 cup onion, chopped
1½ cups carrots, chopped
1½ cups parsnips, chopped
2 ribs celery, chopped

2 to 3 cloves garlic, smashed
2 cups Belgian quad (I like
   St. Bernardus Abt 12)
2 cups chicken stock, or more
   if needed
1 bunch fresh thyme
1 bunch fresh rosemary
2 bay leaves

[PREPARATION]

1. Tie the beef shanks with kitchen twine to secure the meat to the bone.
2. Pat the shanks dry with a paper towel and season both sides with salt and pepper.
3. Dredge the shanks in flour and shake off any excess.
4. In a large ovenproof sauté pan or skillet, cook the pancetta until the fat is rendered. Remove the pancetta from the pan and set aside to add to the sauce later.
5. To the hot pancetta fat, add the shanks and brown on all sides; work in batches to avoid crowding the pan. Remove the shanks and set aside.

continued >

PERFECT PAIRING

Belgian quad-style beers are big, malty, almost sweet beers that often boast a combination of yeasty character and tropical notes. If you can't get the **ST. BERNARDUS** or another quad, go with a rich trippel.

6. Preheat oven to 375°F.

7. To the pan, add the onion, carrot, parsnips, and celery; season with salt. Sauté until the onion is slightly translucent and the vegetables begin to soften. Add the garlic and cook for 1 to 2 minutes.

8. Add the beer to the pan. Nestle the shanks into the beer and top with chicken stock to bring the liquid level just to the top of the shanks. Toss in the thyme, rosemary, and bay leaves.

9. Cover tightly with foil and place in the oven for 1 hour. After an hour has passed, check the liquid level. Add additional chicken stock, if needed, to bring the liquid level three-quarters of the way up the sides of the meat.

10. Cover, return to oven, and cook an additional 30 minutes to an hour. The meat will be tender and falling off of the bone when it is ready.

11. Remove the shanks and tent with foil.

12. Skim the fat off the top of the sauce. Strain out the vegetables, return the sauce to a pan, and boil the sauce to reduce it a bit further. Add the reserved pancetta to the sauce.

13. Serve shanks with the vegetables (remove the bay leaves, thyme, and rosemary stems) and sauce. Great with risotto or garlic mashed potatoes!

PAUL SEGURA'S FAVORITE BIG BEER BURGER
WITH BEER ONIONS AND BEER-BRINED BACON

RECIPE BY GUNTHER EMATHINGER, EXECUTIVE CHEF,
KARL STRAUSS BREWING COMPANY

[serves 4]

For the burgers and marinade:
1 cup Karl Strauss Amber
1 cup Worcestershire sauce
4 tablespoons Dijon mustard
4 tablespoons low-sodium soy
   sauce
4 tablespoons garlic, minced
4 tablespoons shallots, minced
4 tablespoons fresh Italian parsley,
   chopped
2 tablespoons freshly ground black
   pepper
1 teaspoon kosher salt
4 (8-ounce) ground beef patties

For the brined bacon:
2 tablespoons vegetable oil
4 tablespoons garlic, minced
4 tablespoons shallot, minced
4 tablespoons cider vinegar
4 tablespoons granulated sugar
1 teaspoon kosher salt

1 teaspoon freshly ground black
   pepper
2 cups Endless Summer Light
   (or pilsner)
8 strips extra-thick applewood-
   smoked bacon

For the beer onions:
1 tablespoon vegetable oil
1 medium yellow onion, thinly sliced
1 cup Red Trolley Ale (or red ale)
¼ teaspoon kosher salt
¼ teaspoon freshly ground pepper

For the mushrooms:
1 tablespoon vegetable oil
2 cups button mushrooms, sliced
1 tablespoon garlic, minced
½ cup Tower 10 IPA
1 tablespoon parsley, chopped
Salt and black pepper

*Paul Segura, brewmaster for
Karl Strauss Brewing Company,
is a big guy — and he likes big
flavors in his beer and in his food.
That's why this big, bold burger
is perfect for Paul. "This thing
has everything you could possibly
want in a burger — garlic,
onions, spices, bacon, cheese,
mushrooms, and lots of great beer
flavors," Paul says.*

continued >

**PERFECT
PAIRING**

Paul's favorite pairing for this dish is a crisp, hoppy pale ale like his **PINTAIL PALE ALE**, or a great IPA, like **TOWER 10 IPA, TOWER 20 IIPA,** or **KARL STRAUSS'S BIG BARREL DOUBLE IPA.**

Paul Segura:
"In this recipe, Chef Emathinger uses four different beers, each matched to a unique component of the dish. Any burger that uses four different beers is what I'd consider a kick-ass burger."

PAUL SEGURA'S FAVORITE BIG BEER BURGER
continued from page 145

For the bacon spice:
¼ teaspoon smoked paprika
¼ teaspoon freshly ground black pepper
¼ teaspoon chili powder
¼ teaspoon onion powder
¼ teaspoon garlic powder
1 tablespoon granulated sugar
1 tablespoon brown sugar
¼ teaspoon kosher salt

Finishing touches:
4 slices Gruyere cheese
4 large hamburger buns
4 lettuce leaves
4 slices tomato

[PREPARATION]
1. Marinate the burger patties: Mix all the marinade ingredients together in a nonreactive bowl. Add the patties and marinate in the refrigerator for 3 to 4 hours.
2. Make the bacon brine: Heat the oil in a saucepan and sauté the garlic and shallots until translucent. Add the cider vinegar to the pan and stir to scrape up any browned bits. Add the sugar, salt, pepper, and beer. Remove from heat and refrigerate. Once the brine is cool, submerge the bacon slices and refrigerate for 3 hours.
3. Make the bacon spice: Blend all ingredients in a

small bowl, reserve.
4. Make the beer onions: Heat oil in a small saucepan and sauté onions until well browned. Add the Red Trolley Ale and stir to scrape up any browned bits. Add salt and pepper. Cook the onions until all the beer has evaporated. Remove from heat and set aside.
5. Make the mushrooms: Heat oil in a small sauté pan and add the mushrooms and garlic. Sauté until lightly browned and then add the Tower 10 IPA, stirring to scrape up any browned bits. Add the parsley and salt and pepper to taste. Cook the mushrooms until all the beer has evaporated, remove from heat, and set aside.
6. Preheat oven to 350°F.
7. Cook the bacon: Remove bacon from marinade and pat dry with paper towels. Season bacon on both sides with the bacon spice. Place seasoned bacon strips on a slotted broiler pan and bake for 15 to 20 minutes, until crisp. Remove from oven and place bacon on paper towels to drain.
8. Preheat a grill. Remove the burger patties from the marinade and pat dry with paper towels. Season with salt and pepper to taste, and grill almost to desired doneness. During the last 30 seconds of cooking time, top each burger patty with warm beer onions and the Gruyere cheese. Cover burgers with a metal bowl and let cheese melt.
9. In the meantime, toast the buns and place the bottom half of a bun on each serving plate. Place a patty with melted cheese on top of the bun and top with more of the beer onions, mushrooms, lettuce, tomato, beer-brined bacon, and any desired condiments.

CHEF GUNTHER'S POT ROAST SLIDERS
WITH BLACK GARLIC-TRUFFLE HORSERADISH SAUCE

GUNTHER EMATHINGER, EXECUTIVE CHEF, KARL STRAUSS BREWING COMPANY   *[serves 4]*

Chef's Note: *Black garlic is a fermented garlic that has a unique sweet-savory flavor, and is available at some supermarkets, Whole Foods, Jimbo's, and other specialty produce markets.*

For the pot roast:
3 tablespoons vegetable oil
3 pounds boneless chuck roast, well marbled
1½ tablespoons kosher salt
1½ tablespoons freshly ground black pepper
2 medium yellow onions, chopped
3 celery ribs, chopped
9 cloves garlic, chopped
3 cups Fullsuit Belgian Style Brown Ale
⅓ cup balsamic vinegar
¾ cup tomato juice
2 bay leaves

For the sauce:
3 tablespoons vegetable oil

2 yellow onions, thinly sliced
½ pound cremini mushrooms (or button mushrooms)
1 teaspoon garlic, minced
½ tablespoon freshly ground black pepper
½ tablespoon fresh thyme, chopped
1 tablespoon all-purpose flour
1 cup Fullsuit Belgian Style Brown Ale
Salt, to taste

For the horseradish sauce:
½ cup Fullsuit Belgian-style Brown Ale
½ cup water
1 bulb black garlic, skin on
2 tablespoons mayonnaise
¼ cup sour cream

continued >

Chef Gunther calls this recipe "comfort food at its best." The meat is slow-braised in aromatic vegetables and beer to tender perfection before it's slathered in a rich mushroom sauce and topped with a creamy black garlic, truffle oil, and horseradish sauce. "It's a beautiful combination of flavors," Gunther says, "and I love the special dark-fruit flavor that the black garlic adds."

Gunther is a big fan of pairing black garlic with a balanced but malt-forward beer like **RED TROLLEY ALE** or **OFF THE RAILS** (which is the turbo-charged version of **RED TROLLEY ALE**). An English-style brown ale or Belgian-style brown (**KARL'S FULLSUIT BELGIAN STYLE BROWN ALE**) are other great options.

PERFECT PAIRING

CHEF GUNTHER'S POT ROAST SLIDERS

continued from page 147

1 tablespoon prepared horseradish
Dash freshly ground black pepper
½ teaspoon white truffle oil

Finishing touches:
8 slider buns or hot dog buns
8 small slices Gruyere or Gouda cheese
2 tablespoons fresh chives, chopped

[PREPARATION]

1. Prepare the roast: Preheat oven to 225°F. Heat oil in heavy, large ovenproof skillet. Rub the beef with pepper and salt, and sear in the skillet on all sides until well browned. Remove beef and add onions, celery, and garlic to the skillet. Sauté until well browned. Add the beer, vinegar, and tomato juice, and stir to scrape up any browned bits on the bottom of the pan. Bring to a boil, add the bay leaves, and boil until reduced by half. Remove from heat.

2. Add beef and any drippings back to the skillet, cover tightly with a lid or aluminum foil, and put in the oven. Braise for approximately 3 hours, until meat is until fork-tender. Check the roast every 30 minutes. Pot roast should always have about an inch of cooking liquid in the pan. Add hot water as needed. Remove the roast from oven and let it rest in the skillet for about 30 minutes.

3. Remove the roast from the skillet and set aside,

covered, in a warm place until the sauce is finished. Use any accumulated juices from the roast to add to the sauce.

4. Make the sauce: Heat oil in a saucepan and sauté the onions until well browned. Add mushrooms, garlic, pepper, and thyme, and sauté for 5 minutes.

5. Sprinkle the flour over the vegetables and then add the beer to the pan. Scrape up any browned bits from the bottom of the pan and cook until most of the liquid has evaporated. Add the reserved cooking liquid from the roast, bring to a boil, and simmer for 15 minutes.

6. Adjust seasoning with salt and pepper to taste. (The sauce should be the thickness of thick heavy cream at this point. If it's too thick, adjust with water. If it's too thin, continue to cook and reduce.)

7. Remove sauce from heat and set aside.

8. Make the horseradish sauce: Combine the beer and water in small saucepan and bring to a boil. Add the black garlic bulb and simmer for 3 minutes. Remove from heat and let cool in cooking liquid before peeling the garlic cloves.

9. In a small bowl, combine mayonnaise, sour cream, horseradish, pepper, and truffle oil. Coarsely chop three of the black garlic cloves and mix into the sauce.

10. Assemble the sliders: Lightly toast the slider buns and place on a serving plate. Place a slice of cheese on each. Reheat the pot roast sauce in small sauté pan. Break the pot roast into large bite-size pieces and add the pieces to the sauce. Simmer the pot roast until the sauce becomes thick. Divide the pot roast among the sliders and top each with any remaining mushroom and onion sauce. Finish with ½ tablespoon of the horseradish sauce and a sprinkle of chopped chives.

GOULASH AND DUMPLINGS

YUSEFF CHERNEY, HEAD BREWER AND DISTILLER,
BALLAST POINT BREWING & SPIRITS

[serves 6–8]

"We've traveled a lot to the Czech Republic," says Yuseff. "We have relatives there, and goulash is one of those things I tend to eat every day when I'm there. So, it's near and dear to me." Yuseff explains that his recipe has beer in it because, "it's a given. It's what we do. And if you ask anyone in the Czech Republic, they would be flabbergasted to think of doing goulash without beer in it."

For the goulash:
1 to 2 tablespoons olive oil
3 pounds stew beef, cubed
1 pound pork, cubed
1 pound chuck steak, finely cubed
   (the fatty steak breaks down
   during long cooking and adds to
   the mouthfeel)
3 yellow onions, finely sliced
2 green bell peppers, sliced
2 red bell peppers, sliced (reserve
   several slices for garnish)
4 cups beef broth
4 cups chicken broth
1 (28-ounce) can diced tomatoes
1 (6-ounce) can tomato paste
⅓ cup ketchup
4 tablespoons Hungarian paprika
1 tablespoon marjoram
1 tablespoon ground black pepper
¼ teaspoon ground cinnamon
1 teaspoon salt

4 cloves fresh garlic, minced
24 ounces Ballast Point Pale Ale

For the dumplings:
4 eggs
2 cups milk
1 teaspoon salt
½ cup finely chopped parsley
1 large baguette, cut into 1-inch
   cubes
1 tablespoon olive oil
½ onion, cut in small dice
2 tablespoons bread crumbs
1 tablespoon all-purpose flour
1 handful fresh chives, finely
   chopped

Finishing touches:
1 to 2 tablespoons cornstarch
   (if needed to thicken goulash)
6 to 8 pepperoncinis
6 to 8 tablespoons sour cream

continued >

PERFECT PAIRING

Traditional goulashes in Germany or the Czech Republic are commonly paired with some kind of pilsner. At home, Yuseff prefers pairing this with **BALLAST POINT PALE ALE**, which is similar in many ways to a pilsner. "It's a real subtle beer, crisp, and light, so it goes well with this."

[PREPARATION]

1. Make the goulash: Heat some olive oil (1 to 2 tablespoons) in a large skillet on high heat and brown the beef, pork, and chuck steak. (You may need to work in batches so the pan doesn't get too crowded and the meat is able to brown.) Remove browned meat to a large stock pot.

2. In the same skillet, add the onion and cook until translucent. Add to the pot with the meat.

3. In the skillet, cook the red and green bell peppers for 5 minutes. Add to the meat and onions.

4. Add all the remaining goulash ingredients to the pot and bring to a boil. Cook for 20 minutes at a low boil, and then transfer to a crockpot.

5. Cook on high for 2 hours, then switch to low for another 6 hours, or until the meat is fork-tender and falls apart. Gently stir, being careful to avoid breaking the meat apart, as it will be super tender.

6. Make the dumplings: In a bowl, mix together the eggs, milk, salt, and parsley. Add the baguette cubes and let soak for 15 minutes.

7. In a skillet, heat olive oil and cook the diced onions to a golden brown. Add to the baguette mixture, along with the bread crumbs and the flour. Mix well. Add the fresh chives, stirring just to incorporate.

8. Form dumplings in your hands — they should roll into a ball with the consistency of a meatball. (Dumplings will expand while cooking, so start with a ball a little larger than a golf ball.)

9. Fill a large pot with salted water and bring to a boil. Place one dumpling in the boiling water. If it falls apart, add more bread crumbs to the mixture. If consistency is good, add remaining dumplings to the pot and boil for 30 minutes.

10. Finish the goulash: When goulash is done and the meat is fork-tender, thicken the sauce with cornstarch if desired. (In a small bowl, add a little cold water to 1 tablespoon of cornstarch and whisk. Then add to the

goulash and cook for another 20 minutes on low).

11. To serve, ladle goulash into bowls or onto plates and place dumplings on top. Garnish with sliced pepperoncini, sour cream, and fresh red bell pepper.

SWEET GEORGIA BROWN LAMB STEW
ON ROASTED GARLIC MASHED POTATOES

KAREN BLAIR, HAMILTON'S TAVERN, SMALL BAR, ELEVEN,
AND MONKEY PAW BAR PUB & BREWERY

[serves 4]

"This recipe came about from a Greek-themed menu we did at Hamilton's," Karen recalls. *"You find a lot lot of lamb in Greek cuisine, and I love stews — I make them all the time. Anything with gravy and potatoes is pretty much my thing."*

For the potatoes:
¼ cup olive oil
1 head garlic
6 white potatoes, peeled and cut into chunks
¼ cup heavy cream
3 tablespoons unsalted butter
Kosher salt and coarsely ground pepper, to taste

For the stew:
3 pounds lamb shoulder, cut into chunks and patted dry

½ cup all-purpose flour
Olive oil
½ yellow onion, diced
1 teaspoon kosher salt
1 teaspoon coarsely ground pepper
2 cloves garlic, chopped
½ teaspoon dried Mediterranean oregano
1 to 2 large carrots, diced
1 cup Monkey Paw Sweet Georgia Brown (or any great, malty brown)
1 cup fresh English peas (frozen peas work, too!)

[PREPARATION]
1. Preheat oven to 400°F.
2. Start the potatoes: Pour the olive oil into one of the wells of a cupcake pan. Cut the garlic head in half, exposing all the bulbs. Discard the tops. Add the garlic to the oil, cover with foil, and poach in the oven for about 1 hour.

continued >

PERFECT PAIRING

If you live in San Diego and love craft beer, you know who Scot Blair is. He owns four of the city's most popular beer spots, including Monkey Paw (his newest), which is located downtown. One of the things that sets Monkey Paw apart from its sister bars is that it's also a brewery. The bar's signature brown ale, **SWEET GEORGIA BROWN**, is a wonderfully malty beer with a rich mouthfeel and a creamy head.

3. Start the stew: Dredge the lamb lightly in flour.

4. In a large pot, heat 2 tablespoons olive oil over medium heat. When the oil is hot, add lamb and brown on all sides. Work in batches if necessary to avoid crowding the lamb. Add more olive oil as needed. Transfer the lamb to a bowl and cover with foil.

5. Add onion to the pot and season with salt and pepper. Stir frequently to avoid burning. Cook onion until soft and lightly browned. Add the garlic and stir, cooking for 30 seconds more.

6. Return the meat to the pot and add the oregano, carrots, and beer. Bring to a simmer, cooking until slightly reduced, but do not boil. Add 1 cup water and bring the pot back to a simmer for 30 minutes to thicken the gravy. Add peas and simmer for another 30 minutes. Taste and adjust seasoning, if necessary.

7. Bring a pot of water with 1 teaspoon salt to a boil and add the potatoes. Cook until soft, about 20 minutes. Drain immediately.

8. Return potatoes to the pot and add the cream, butter, salt, pepper, and poached garlic cloves, which have been squeezed out of the skin (use the garlicky olive oil for something else). With a hand mixer on low, mash potatoes, increasing the speed as the ingredients are incorporated. Adjust seasoning with salt and pepper to taste.

9. Serve stew over mashed potatoes.

IMPERIAL STOUT POT ROAST

A.G. WARFIELD, EXECUTIVE CHEF, CHURCHILL'S PUB & GRILLE   *[serves 4–6]*

For the pot roast:
4 tablespoons canola oil or olive oil
3 pounds beef chuck roast
Salt and pepper, to taste
2 white onions, diced
1 bunch celery, chopped
2 bunches carrots, chopped, tops reserved
6 cloves garlic, smashed
1 cup shallots, diced

4 cups beef stock
22 ounces imperial stout (I like Lagunitas Imperial Stout)
3 pounds red potatoes, quartered
3 bay leaves

Finishing touches:
Fresh carrot tops, chopped
Fresh scallions, chopped
Fresh parsley, chopped
Grilled French bread

[PREPARATION]

1. Preheat oven to 350°F. Heat the oil to near smoking in a roasting pan. Generously season the meat with salt and pepper, and sear on all sides. (The pan should be smoking hot!) Cook about 3 to 5 minutes, until the meat is golden brown on one side, and then turn it and brown the other side.

2. After browning the meat, add the onion, celery, carrot, garlic, and shallots. Sauté for 5 minutes, and add the stock, stout, potatoes, and bay leaves. Cover tightly with foil and cook for 3 hours, turning the roast after 1½ hours.

3. Serve a portion of meat with potato and carrots, top with sauce, and garnish with carrot tops, scallions, and fresh parsley. Grilled French bread also makes a great accompaniment.

A.G. says this dish "goes great with a nice stout or porter, such as **ALESMITH'S SPEEDWAY STOUT, BLACK LIGHTNING PORTER, CORONADO'S STOOPID STOUT,** or **IRON FIST'S VELVET GLOVE**." A.G. loves the way the slow braise with stout "brings out all these beautiful characteristics" in the meat and the vegetables.

PERFECT PAIRING

Churchill's is one of the region's best-loved beer bars, located right in the heart of San Marcos — one of the county's most brewery-rich areas. Naturally, Churchill's chef, A.G. Warfield, likes to do a lot with beer on his menu. He was inspired to do this recipe "one cold night when I was in the grocery store and I happened to pick up a bottle of Speedway Stout. Then I saw that chuck roast was on sale. I went from there. "Low and slow, that's the secret to this dish."

RITUAL'S PERFECT PORK BELLY
WITH GLAZED CARROTS AND PARSNIP PURÉE

ADRIAN RAMIREZ, CHEF, RITUAL TAVERN   *[serves 6–8]*

*"I've always loved doing duck confit,"
explains Chef Adrian Ramirez
(center, with Ritual Tavern owner
Michael Flores, left, and New
English Brewing Company founder
Simon Lacey), "but when I thought
about creating a recipe that would
pair well with beer, I naturally
thought of pork." So, Adrian just put
the two ideas together and created
a dish that cooks pork belly like a
confit (which means in some kind of
fat). The secret to making this dish
successfully, as Adrian explains, is
"patience."*

Chef's Note: *This recipe is best when the rubbed pork is refrigerated for 24 hours and the cooked pork is cooled again overnight.*

For the rub cure:
5 pounds pork belly
½ cup kosher salt
½ cup brown sugar
1 cup white wine, reduced by half

For cooking the pork:
1 head whole garlic
6 sprigs fresh thyme
3 bay leaves
2 fresh rosemary sprigs
10 black peppercorns
2 pounds duck fat, or 2 to 4 cups
  soybean oil, enough to cover
  pork (duck fat is available at
  Iowa Meat Farms)

For the glazed carrots:
2 pounds baby carrots, rinsed

well, stalks broken off
(leave on a bit of the green
top)
2 ounces Brewers Special
  Brown Ale
4 tablespoons butter
¼ cup brown sugar
Salt and freshly ground pepper,
  to taste

For the parsnip purée:
2 pounds parsnips, peeled and
  sliced lengthwise
1 tablespoon butter
½ cup heavy cream
½ cup milk
2 pinches ground nutmeg
Salt and freshly ground pepper,
  to taste

continued >

PERFECT PAIRING

Chef Ramirez created this dish to pair with one of his favorite beers, the **BREWERS SPECIAL BROWN ALE**. Simon Lacey, New English Brewing Company's owner and brewer, likes to say he "makes great English-style beers that have a West Coast flair." That means most of his beers pull back on the hops in favor of malt-forward flavors that make them perfect for cooking.

[PREPARATION]

1. Rub the pork: Thoroughly coat the pork belly with salt and brown sugar. In a baking pan or casserole dish just barely big enough to hold the meat, pour the reduced white wine. Place the pork belly on top of the liquid. Cover tightly with plastic wrap and refrigerate for 24 hours.

2. Preheat oven to 275°F.

3. Rinse the pork, pat dry, and return it to the baking pan. Cut the whole head of garlic in half and place the halves in the baking dish along with the thyme, bay leaves, rosemary, and peppercorns.

4. Spread enough room temperature duck fat to just barely cover the pork belly. (Traditional confit calls for duck or pig fat, but soybean oil is a good alternative.) Place in the oven and cook for 4 to 6 hours. The pork belly is done when a fork stuck into the meat releases easily without moving the pork around in its liquid. The pork belly is ready to serve at this point, but if you have the time, you can maximize the flavor and tenderness with an additional cure: Allow the baking pan to cool and place the entire contents in the refrigerator overnight. The fat cap will effectively seal the dish as it cools.

5. When ready to serve, preheat oven to 350°F and remove the pork from the baking dish.

6. Make the carrots: In a saucepan, bring 3 quarts of water to a boil. Lower the heat and blanch the carrots for 3 minutes. Drain the carrots and immediately immerse them in cold water to stop the cooking.

7. Put the brown ale in a sauté pan and simmer for 2 minutes. Add the butter and sugar, and stir until the butter and sugar melt. Add the carrots and cook until the glaze thickens. Season with salt and pepper and set aside.

8. Make the parsnips: In a large saucepan, bring 4 quarts of water to a boil and add the parsnips. When the parsnips are soft enough to be easily mashed, drain them and and place them in a large bowl. Add the butter,

cream, and milk, and mash thoroughly. Season with nutmeg and salt and pepper to taste. Keep warm.

9. Reheat the pork by placing it, fat side down, in a hot skillet for 3 minutes. Flip the pork over so the fat side is up, then transfer to the oven for 15 minutes. Slice into pork into portions and place each piece on top of a mound of parsnip purée, with carrots on the side.

MATT RATTNER'S FAVORITE BBQ CARNITAS PIZZA

RECIPE BY GUNTHER EMATHINGER, EXECUTIVE CHEF,
KARL STRAUSS BREWING COMPANY

[makes 4 personal pizzas]

Everyone at Karl Strauss agrees that Executive Chef Gunther Emathinger is a wizard in the kitchen when it comes to developing great recipes with beer. This recipe is a particular favorite of brewery co-founder and co-owner Matt Rattner (pictured), who "loves the way the spiciness blends with the beer, and the beer brings out the sweet smokiness in the meat." Because this recipe is actually three sub-recipes combined, you can also use the dough for a different pizza, and add the delicious BBQ sauce to another dish.

For the pork:
2 pounds boneless pork shoulder
1 tablespoon dried oregano
½ tablespoon ground cumin
8 tablespoons vegetable oil, divided use
2 chipotle peppers canned in adobo, coarsely chopped
6 cloves garlic, minced
1½ tablespoons salt
1½ tablespoons freshly ground black pepper
1 onion, coarsely chopped
1 medium jalapeño, coarsely chopped*
1 orange, juiced
1½ cups Red Trolley Ale

For the dough:
½ envelope dry yeast
¾ cup Amber Lager (¼ cup room temperature, ½ cup chilled)
1 cup bread flour, plus additional

flour for stretching the dough
1 cup all-purpose flour
1 tablespoon granulated sugar
1½ teaspoons kosher salt
2 tablespoons olive oil, plus extra for oiling the bowl

For the BBQ sauce:
3 tablespoons vegetable oil
½ cup onion, cut in small dice
¼ cup green bell peppers, cut in small dice
1 tablespoon garlic, minced
3 cups ketchup (preferably Heinz)
½ cup yellow mustard
¾ cup brown sugar
½ cup honey
¼ cup cider vinegar
2 tablespoons Worcestershire sauce
1 tablespoon chili powder
1 tablespoon smoked paprika

continued >

PERFECT PAIRING

KARL STRAUSS AMBER and **RED TROLLEY ALE** are both excellent partners for this pizza, if you want to accent the malty, bready aspects of the dish. If you want something crisper to cut the fattiness of the pork and to offset the spice, **TOWER 10 IPA** is your choice.

MATT RATTNER'S FAVORITE BBQ CARNITAS PIZZA

continued from page 158

For the chile-beer infusion:

5 ounces dried ancho chiles, stems and seeds removed
2 cups Red Trolley Ale

For the topping (on each pizza):

3 ounces shredded low-moisture mozzarella cheese
1 medium jalapeño pepper, sliced thinly into rounds*
1 medium red jalapeño pepper, sliced thinly into rounds*
1 ounce red onion, thinly sliced
1½ ounces crumbled goat cheese
1 tablespoon fresh cilantro, coarsely chopped

[PREPARATION]

1. Prepare the pork: Preheat oven to 325°F. Rinse pork and pat dry with paper towels. Combine oregano, cumin, 2 tablespoons of vegetable oil, chipotle peppers, garlic, salt and pepper, and rub all over the pork.

2. Place pork in a deep-sided baking dish and top with the chopped onions and jalapeños. Add the orange juice and Red Trolley Ale, and cover tightly with aluminum foil. Bake for 2 to 3 hours until meat is fork tender.

3. Make the dough: Sprinkle the yeast over the room-temperature Amber Lager and stir to dissolve. Let stand for about 15 minutes in a warm place.

4. In the bowl of a mixer, combine the flours, sugar, salt, and oil, and mix on low speed for 30 seconds.

5. Add the yeast mixture and cold beer, and mix on low speed until dough comes together. Increase the speed slightly and knead the dough until it is smooth and begins to pull away from the sides of the bowl (about 8 minutes).

6. Place the dough on floured surface and knead by hand for another 1 to 2 minutes. Use additional flour for dusting to prevent sticking. Shape the dough into a large ball and place into a lightly oiled bowl covered loosely with plastic wrap. Let it rise to about double in size (about 1 hour).

7. Make the BBQ sauce: Heat oil in large sauté pan and sauté the onions, peppers, and garlic on medium heat until translucent. Add all remaining ingredients, stirring well, and bring the sauce to a boil. Reduce heat and simmer for about 15 minutes.

8. Remove sauce from heat and cool. Then blend in a food processor until smooth. (Adjust the thickness of sauce with water. It should be like thick cream.) Adjust seasoning with salt and pepper, and refrigerate.

9. Make the chile-beer infusion: Place the ancho chiles in a small saucepan with the Red Trolley Ale and simmer until the chiles are soft and the beer is reduced by half. Remove from the heat and set aside.

10. Divide the dough: After the dough has risen, divide into 4 equal pieces and gently knead each piece. Form each into a ball, set it on a lightly oiled baking sheet, and cover with plastic wrap. Let dough rest for about 30 minutes.

11. Roll out each dough ball with a rolling pin on a lightly floured surface into a 10- to 12-inch circle. Lightly dust the rolled dough with flour, cover loosely with a clean towel, and repeat with the remaining balls.

12. Finish the pork: When the pork is done, remove it from the baking dish and let it cool. Pull it apart into small chunks. Heat remaining oil in a large sauté pan, and fry the pork pieces until brown and crisp. Remove browned pieces from oil and drain on paper towels.

13. Preheat a pizza stone in a 450°F oven.

14. Assemble the pizzas: Combine the ancho-beer infusion with the BBQ sauce and spread some to cover each pizza, leaving about a half-inch border. Next, evenly sprinkle the mozzarella and top with about ½ cup of the pork, jalapeños, onion, and goat cheese. Place pizza carefully on the pizza stone and bake until edges turn brown, about 10 minutes. Remove from the oven, sprinkle with cilantro, and cut into 8 equal slices.

Note: Wear gloves when chopping peppers, and avoid touching your eyes.

AVANT GARDE HERB-CRUSTED LAMB MEDALLIONS
WITH AVANT GARDE WHIPPED POTATOES

KEVIN HOPKINS, HOSPITALITY MANAGER, PORT BREWING AND THE LOST ABBEY   *[serves 4]*

Chef's Note: *Lamb is best when allowed to marinate for 6 to 24 hours.*

For the lamb:
8 lamb loin chops
2 cups Avant Garde
Olive oil
Salt and pepper

For the potatoes:
4 tablespoons kosher salt
¾ cup sweet onion, diced
8 cloves garlic, minced
5 large russet baking potatoes
1 stick (½ cup) unsalted butter,
　cubed
½ teaspoon freshly ground black
　pepper
¼ teaspoon cayenne pepper
1 to 1½ cups sour cream
¼ cup fresh chives, cut to ½-inch
　lengths
½ cup Avant Garde

For the herb coating:
1½ cups plain bread crumbs
½ cup grated Parmesan cheese
2 to 3 large sprigs fresh rosemary,
　leaves removed
6 sprigs fresh thyme, leaves
　removed
2 cloves garlic, minced
½ cup fresh parsley, chopped
1 to 2 teaspoons olive oil
¾ cup Dijon mustard
4 tablespoons Avant Garde
Sea salt and freshly ground black
　pepper, to taste

Finishing touches:
Smoked paprika
Fresh thyme or rosemary
sprigs

continued >

Kevin Hopkins, who is a world traveled cook, is a long-time lamb lover, and he's actually done many variations of this recipe in the past. A few years ago, he started marinating the meat in beer, and he loved the results. "The beer takes away some of the gaminess of lamb," Kevin says. "It also tenderizes the meat and really brightens it up."

AVANT GARDE is a bier de garde, or farmhouse-style ale. It's a clean, well-balanced ale (fermented with lager yeast) that has comforting flavors of biscuits, caramel, and fresh-baked bread. The relative crispness and medium body of this beer is a great counterpoint to the richness of the lamb.

PERFECT PAIRING

Kevin Hopkins: "I wanted a recipe where the beer really comes through in the finished dish. Too many recipes have beer in them, but you can't taste the beer! That's why I put varying amounts of beer in the marinade, the mustard, and the potatoes."

AVANT GARDE HERB-CRUSTED LAMB MEDALLIONS

continued from page 161

[PREPARATION]

1. Prepare the lamb: Trim the chops so there is minimal fat along the edges. Put the chops in a zipper-top plastic bag or other sealable container and add 2 cups of beer, making sure the meat is covered well. (Add water if additional liquid is needed.) Refrigerate and marinate for a minimum of 30 minutes, though 6 to 24 hours is optimal. Remove the lamb from refrigerator at least 2 hours before cooking.

2. Preheat oven to 400°F.

3. Start the potatoes: Fill a large stockpot with water and place on high heat. (Make sure there is enough water to cover the potatoes by about 2 inches.) Add kosher salt, diced sweet onion, and minced garlic. Bring to a rolling boil. Wash, peel, and cube the potatoes, removing any blemishes, while the water heats.

4. In a large oven-safe pan, heat enough olive oil to sear the lamb. Remove the lamb from the marinade, pat dry with a paper towel, and generously season with salt and pepper on both sides. When oil is almost smoking, place lamb in pan and brown all sides. Do not overcook. Place pan in oven and bake for 7 minutes. (Leave the oven on when you take the lamb out.)

5. Cook the potatoes: When water is ready, add potatoes, stir well, and boil 12 to 15 minutes or until a sharp knife can be inserted into the center of a potato without forcing, but not too easily. (Think baked potato consistency. Potatoes should not be soggy or come apart in the pot.) Drain thoroughly. (Careful! Potatoes go from almost done to overdone very quickly!)

6. Make the crust: Combine bread crumbs, Parmesan, rosemary, thyme, garlic, and parsley in a food processor. Add a small amount of olive oil to bind and pulse until you have an evenly combined mixture. Spread the mixture on a plate. Crust should be a fine crumble but not wet.

7. Combine mustard and the Avant Garde in a small bowl and set aside.

8. Brush lamb with beer mustard on top and sides and coat evenly with crumb mixture. Put chops back in pan, crust side up, and set aside until potatoes are finished.

9. Finish the potatoes: Melt butter in a stockpot and add drained potatoes. Grind/sprinkle black pepper and cayenne evenly over potatoes and add sour cream. Using a hand mixer on medium speed, incorporate ingredients while ensuring that the potatoes are broken down to an even consistency. There should be no chunks or cubes left, but do not over mix. Potatoes should be pasty.

10. Adjust seasoning with salt, if needed. Add chives and ½ cup of Avant Garde. With the mixer on high, whip the potatoes, blending thoroughly. Mixture should be smooth with stiff peaks (like a good meringue), and chives should be mixed evenly throughout. (Add more beer and/or sour cream if additional liquid is needed to achieve a smooth and creamy — but not soft — consistency.) Cover potatoes to keep them warm.

11. Just before serving, put lamb back in oven for an additional 8 to 10 minutes to reheat and tighten up crumb topping. (Or you can place them under a broiler for 4 to 5 minutes, until crust just starts to brown).

12. To serve, stir the potatoes and place an oval mound on each plate. Sprinkle lightly with smoked paprika. Rest chops together on potatoes and garnish with sprigs of thyme or rosemary. If you want a vegetable accompaniment, baby carrots oven-roasted in aged balsamic vinegar, or another non-green seasonal vegetable of choice, would be great.

Hosting Your Own Beer Dinner:
Ideas and Inspirations

Whipping up a buttery parsnip purée...

There are lots of excellent reasons to host your own beer dinner. For one, it's a great way to explore the magic of pairing beer and food. It's a great way to taste a range of beers (perhaps some you've never tasted before). And it's a great way to spend quality time with a group of your favorite friends or family.

One of the goals of a good beer dinner is to explore the relationship between certain beers and certain foods. Often at a beer dinner you'll first taste a beer and get a feeling for its flavors. Then you'll taste the food it's paired with and get a sense of those flavors. Then you'll taste the BEER AND THE FOOD TOGETHER, and (hopefully) they will both be elevated to a new level. Each will complement or contrast flavors and characteristics you hadn't noticed before, and the marriage of the food and the beer will create a special taste experience.

One thing a beer dinner should not be is stuffy. It should not be overly structured or stressful for the hosts. The ideas and inspirations we're suggesting here are simply

Good food, good beer, good friends, and good conversation — that's what it's all about. Opposite page, top: Tyson Blake, Ryan Lamb, and Brandon Hernández, making sure all the beers are "good enough to drink."

meant to spark your interest and provide whatever level of guidance you want in considering a beer dinner of your own. Feel free to structure beer dinners however you and your friends like them — there is no right or wrong way.

There is a group of beer-loving chefs and foodies in San Diego that call themselves The Trenchermen. Most of these guys are professional chefs, but one is a professional brewer and another is a food writer. On a regular basis (usually monthly), The Trenchermen get together to create incredible multi-course dinners that utilize and feature

their favorite beers. The dinners always feature a wide range of beer styles and recipes — they are frequently rather long affairs, and they are always relaxed and fun. In this special section, we'll look at how The Trenchermen go about planning and putting together a great beer dinner.

Step 1: Which beers do you want to feature?
The first step in conceiving your beer dinner is to decide which beers are going to star in the event. The Trenchermen are fond of choosing a specific brewery

and then picking a variety of beers from that lineup. The menu that we're featuring here began with the idea of highlighting the great beers of Ballast Point Brewing & Spirits. Each of the Trenchermen chose a beer (or beers) that he wanted to feature. Then they all decided who would be responsible for which part of the menu. "We are all huge Ballast Point fans," explains Trencherman Nate Soroko. "They do such a full range of styles and flavors, and their beers are all super food-friendly." It doesn't hurt, of course, that Ballast Point's Specialty Brewer, Colby Chandler, is also a member of the group. That means the chefs tend to have access to some pretty special BP beers as well as all the regular brews from throughout the year.

Step 2: Choose or create recipes that will showcase your beers. Complement or contrast?

When it comes to pairing beer and food (or wine and food), there are two basic options for each pairing: Do you want to complement or contrast?

Some beers have subtle aromas or flavor notes (peppery grains of paradise or banana and clove) that can be coaxed out by a complementary food that also has those components. Pairing a chocolate cake with a malty, chocolatey stout or porter is a good example of complementary pairing.

If contrast is your goal, take the main flavor components of the beer and think about ways to play off those elements. If a beer has a lot of hoppy crispness and bitterness, then think about foods that do well paired with high-acid components, such as fatty meats, cheeses, and spicy, rich sauces.

"When I taste a beer, I think about what foods or flavors it reminds me of," says Trencherman Tyson Blake. "If a beer has citrus notes, like grapefruit or orange, I'll think, okay, what are recipes that feature or use citrus? If I want to do some contrasting, I'll think about what sorts of recipes offset citrus well, like fish or salads."

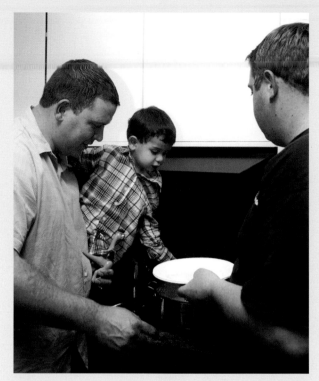

Chefs Tyson Blake (left) and Brandon Brooks consult with tiny chef Max Blake as a dish comes together.

Of course, there's always the option of pairing each dish with more than one beer — maybe one that complements and one that contrasts. Or maybe you want to feature two that complement in different ways or two that contrast in different ways. The choices are endless — so experiment and explore!

Step 3: Schedule a night and plan out your prep.

There's nothing worse than planning an ambitious menu, leaving everything to the last minute, and then spending the entire evening stressed out in the kitchen trying to get everything done. That's why good prep is key to any great beer dinner. The best strategy is to construct a chart on a

From left: Brandon Hernández, Tyson Blake, and Colby Chandler put the finishing touches on Colby's crostini.

piece of paper that lists what can be done 3 days ahead of time, 2 days ahead of time, the day before, and the day of the event. If you're smart about this, you'll see that a good deal of your food can be prepped ahead of time. A lot of recipes (many in this book) require some do-ahead a day or two before serving, but the steps you do in advance often save a good deal of time right before you want to eat.

Step 4: Get your ingredients, start prepping, have fun!
On the following pages is the menu for a four-course beer dinner The Trenchermen held at Colby Chandler's house. The chefs devised these recipes so they would be relatively easy for the average home cook and would also highlight some special aspects of the beers that were paired. Go ahead and give them a try!

SAN DIEGO CROSTINI
WITH ELDER FLOWER CREAM CHEESE, SAGE PESTO, AND LOCAL SMOKED YELLOWTAIL

COLBY CHANDLER, SPECIALTY BREWER, BALLAST POINT BREWING & SPIRITS

[makes 30 crostini appetizers]

Colby Chandler chose to start this menu off with a full-on complementary pairing. His recipe, which he also calls his San Diego Crostini, is a kind of food equivalent of the flavors he puts into the beer he pairs with it. "I use elder flowers to infuse the vodka because we use elderberries and elder flowers in the San Salvador Saison," Colby explains. "I use local fish, in this case smoked yellowtail, and the fried sage leaf and the sage pesto reflect the sage and the pine nuts we also use in the beer." Colby likes to call this kind of recipe development for a beer "finding the bridge flavors" that enhance the elements of both the food and the beer at the same time.

Chef's Notes: *This recipe requires an infusion of vodka that should be made a minimum of 4 days in advance. Also, any kind of smoked fish will do. I really like using a local fish for this dish, since we are pairing it with a beer made with local ingredients. Smoked yellowtail, halibut, or salmon are also good choices.*

For the cream cheese:
½ ounce dried elder flowers
1 cup Ballast Point Fugu Vodka
12 ounces cream cheese, room temperature

For the pesto:
1 cup toasted pine nuts
1 cup Italian parsley, packed
1 cup cilantro, packed
¾ cup sage leaves, packed
¾ cup freshly grated Parmigiano-Reggiano cheese
6 cloves roasted garlic, crushed
¼ to ½ cup extra virgin olive oil (depending on desired thickness)
Salt, to taste

1½ tablespoons freshly squeezed lemon juice

For the fried sage leaves:
2 cups oil, for frying
35 fresh sage leaves

For the crostini:
15 (¼- to ½-inch-thick) slices whole-grain bread with good texture
3 tablespoons unsalted butter, melted
12 ounces smoked yellowtail or other fish, skin removed, cut into 1-inch squares

Finishing touch:
Lemon zest

PERFECT PAIRING

Colby paired his dish with **BALLAST POINT'S SUMMER SAN SALVADOR SAISON** because he used many of the key flavoring ingredients from the beer as key ingredients in the dish.

continued >

[PREPARATION]

1. Infuse the vodka: Place the elder flowers in an airtight container and cover with the vodka. Seal and store for 4 days.

2. Make the pesto (can be done 1 to 2 days in advance): Place the pine nuts, parsley, cilantro, sage, cheese, and garlic in a food processor and process until coarsely puréed. With the machine running, add the olive oil in a slow, steady stream until the pesto reaches a thick but moist consistency. Stir in the salt and lemon juice. Refrigerate until ready to use.

3. Finish the cream cheese: Strain the vodka using a coffee filter placed in a funnel over a large glass. Place the cream cheese in the bowl of an electric mixer. Add the vodka and whip until it is fully incorporated. Place in covered container and chill until ready to use.

4. Fry the sage leaves: In a skillet over medium-high heat, heat the oil to 365°F. Add the sage leaves one at a time, using a metal spatula to keep them separate. Fry until the leaves start to change color. Use a slotted spoon to transfer the leaves to a paper plate lined with paper towels. Set aside until ready to use.

5. Preheat oven to broil. Use a 2-inch round cutter (or the mouth of a beer festival taster glass) to cut 2 to 3 rounds out of each slice of bread. Brush one side of each round with butter and place (butter side up) on a pan lined with parchment paper. Broil until brown and well toasted, about 1 to 2 minutes. Remove from oven, set aside, and let cool.

6. Assemble the crostini: Arrange the bread rounds on a serving platter. Use a piping bag to apply the cream cheese to each round. Place a sage leaf atop the cream cheese and top it with a piece of fish. Spoon a small portion of the pesto on top of the fish, garnish with lemon zest, and serve.

CHILE WAHOO WHEAT MIXTA CEVICHE ON DUCK-FAT TORTILLAS

BRANDON BROOKS, EXECUTIVE CHEF, SOL MARKETS

[serves 4-6 as a second course]

Chef's Note: *This recipe requires a minimum of 4 hours marinating time for the fish. You can also make your own Chile Wahoo Wheat by infusing a 64-ounce growler with 1 or 2 hot chiles of your choice and letting them steep for a day or two. Taste the beer after 12 or 24 hours to check on the heat level, and when desired flavor is achieved, remove the chiles.*

For the fish mix:
½ pound fish, such as yellowtail or rock fish, cut into ½-inch pieces
½ pound shrimp, peeled, deveined, and cut into ½-inch pieces
½ pound bay scallops, whole
8 lemons, juiced
1 grapefruit, juiced
4 tangerines, juiced
22 ounces Ballast Point Chile Wahoo Wheat (or any great wheat beer)

For the sauce:
1 (6-ounce) can tomato paste
½ cup water
½ cup rice wine vinegar
2 lemons, juiced
6 tablespoons horseradish

1 tablespoon salt
2 tablespoons granulated sugar

For the vegetables:
1 tablespoon garlic, minced
3 onions, cut in small dice
6 vine-ripe tomatoes, cut in small dice
2 hot-house cucumbers, cut in small dice
4 jalapeños, seeded and finely diced
2 bunches of cilantro, finely chopped

Finishing touches:
Avocado slices
Cilantro sprigs

continued >

The second course, created by Brandon Brooks, is a study in subtle contrasts. His ceviche mixta *(mixed seafood)* features local rockfish, a mix of scallops and shrimp, and a corn tortilla fried in duck fat. Sweetness *(from the shrimp and scallops)* and the richness of the duck-fat tortilla are two of the major components Brandon was seeking to offset with a crisp, lighter-style beer that shows a good amount of maltiness — but not too much. The spiciness of the beer was also offset by the coolness of the fish and the cold crunch of the vegetables. "The keys to a great ceviche are, first using the freshest, best-quality fish you can find," Brandon explains. "The second key is to mix in a variety of citrus, not just lemon or lime. And, third, salt it properly."

PERFECT PAIRING

BALLAST POINT'S CHILE WAHOO WHEAT is a great pairing for this because it's light and crisp enough to pair well with a cold, light dish but also spicy and hoppy enough to contrast the sweetness of the sauce and the fishes that were used.

> *"There are so many flavors you can add to a dish by adding beer,"* says Brandon Brooks, *"the possibilities are almost endless."*

CHILE WAHOO WHEAT CEVICHE

continued from page 171

[PREPARATION]

1. Prepare the fish mix: In a nonreactive bowl, combine the fish, shrimp, and scallops with the citrus juice and beer. Cover and refrigerate for at least 4 hours and up to 24 hours.

2. Prepare the sauce: Combine all the ingredients in a medium bowl and mix thoroughly. Refrigerate until needed.

3. Prepare the vegetables: Combine the garlic, onion, tomatoes, cucumbers, jalapeños, and cilantro in a large bowl and mix well.

4. When ready to serve, combine the sauce with the vegetables and the marinated fish in a serving bowl and season with salt and pepper to taste. Garnish with avocado slices and cilantro sprigs, and serve immediately.

GRILLED LAMB CHOPS
WITH PURÉED PARSNIPS, GLAZED CARROTS, AND BLACKBERRY SAUCE

NATE SOROKO, HEAD CHEF, TORONADO SAN DIEGO

[serves 6-8]

For the marinade:
2 garlic cloves, minced
4 to 6 sprigs fresh rosemary
4 to 6 sprigs fresh thyme
Salt and freshly ground black
    pepper, to taste
3 tablespoons olive oil
1 lemon, juiced
8 lamb chops (about 3 pounds)

For the parsnip purée:
2 to 3 pounds parsnips, peeled
    and cubed
1 pound butter, cut into pieces
Salt and white pepper, to taste

For the sauce:
1 cup veal or beef stock
½ cup puréed blackberries
    (1 pint fresh)

For the glazed carrots:
2 tablespoons granulated sugar
2 tablespoons apple cider vinegar
    or balsamic vinegar
3 to 4 heirloom carrots, peeled
    and thinly sliced on the bias

Finishing touches:
Edible flowers

[PREPARATION]
1. Make the marinade: in a small bowl, combine all the non-meat ingredients well. Put lamb chops in a zipper-top bag (or the smallest container that will fit them) and add the marinade. Marinate, refrigerated, for a minimum of 1 hour and up to 24 hours. **continued >**

BALLAST POINT'S SOUR WENCH is a Berlinerweiss-style beer that's got major notes of dark fruit at its center. It's crisp, light, and refreshing and will cut through fatty, spicy foods very well.

PERFECT PAIRING

"I love sour beers," says Nate Soroko, "and Ballast Point makes some of my all-time favorites." Nate explains, "Whenever I do a beer dinner, I try to get at least one sour beer pairing onto the menu." This recipe features a nice contrast between the fatty lamb and the sour acidity of the beer. It also includes the "bridge flavor" of the blackberry in the sauce, which echoes the beer's dark fruit flavors.

GRILLED LAMB CHOPS
continued from page 173

2. Make the parsnip purée: Boil the parsnips until they are soft and fork-tender, about 20 minutes. Purée in a food processor and strain, or pass them through a sieve or food mill. Mix in the butter until well incorporated. Season to taste with salt and pepper and set aside, covered, to stay warm.

3. Make the sauce: In a small saucepan on medium heat, place the stock and the blackberry purée. Cook, stirring occasionally, until reduced by one-third. You should have about 1 cup of sauce. Reduce heat to low and keep the sauce warm.

4. Preheat a grill to high.

5. Make the glazed carrots: In a medium bowl, mix the sugar and the vinegar. Add the carrots and toss to coat evenly.

Heat a medium pan on medium-high heat and sauté the carrots until they are flexible but not soft, about 10 minutes. Remove from heat and set aside, covered, to stay warm.

6. Grill the lamb chops to desired doneness (3 to 4 minutes per side for medium).

7. Serve the chops on top of the parsnip purée, with carrots alongside. Drizzle the chops with sauce.

ORANGE SCULPIN CAKE WITH ORANGE-MANGO SEMIFREDDO

TYSON BLAKE, GENERAL MANAGER, O'BRIEN'S PUB

[serves 8-12]

Tyson Blake wanted to create a dessert for this beer menu that would be something of the unexpected — an eye-opener in terms of complementary and contrasting flavors. "Most people don't think of IPAs as dessert beers," Tyson says. "But the citrus qualities and the hoppy bitterness of IPAs make them a great choice for pairing with sweet desserts." Tyson chose to create a dish that would showcase both the citrus and the hoppy elements, and he chose to use Sculpin in the actual recipe as well. This pairing is a surprisingly perfect contrast of sweet and bitter, with citrus bridge flavors in the cake that tie into the citrus elements of the beer.

For the semifreddo:
3 large egg whites
1 cup heavy whipping cream
½ cup granulated sugar
6 large egg yolks
1 orange, juiced and zested
2 mangoes, peeled and puréed

For the cake:
2 cups all-purpose flour
2 teaspoons baking powder
1 cup granulated sugar
1 teaspoon ground cinnamon

2 oranges, juiced and zested
2 eggs
⅓ cup milk

For the syrup:
2 oranges, juiced
¾ cup granulated sugar
⅓ cup Ballast Point Sculpin

Finishing touches:
Mangoes, diced
Strawberries, diced

[PREPARATION]

1. Make the semifreddo: In a mixing bowl using an electric mixer, beat the egg whites until firm peaks form, and refrigerate.

2. In another mixing bowl, beat the cream and ¼ cup of the sugar until firm peaks form, and refrigerate.

3. In a large glass or stainless steel bowl set over a pot of simmering water, beat the yolks and the rest of the sugar until thickened, about 3 to 5 minutes. (Be careful to regulate the temperature so the eggs don't get too hot and cook.) The yolk mixture should be thick enough to coat the back of a spoon. Remove from heat and beat in the orange zest and juice, mixing for another 3 to 5 minutes.

continued >

PERFECT PAIRING

This dessert is all about thinking of IPAs in a whole new light — so you've got to pair this cake with an IPA! **BALLAST POINT'S SCULPIN IPA** is an ideal choice, for the wonderful citrus flavors and tropical aromas it gets from its hops, but any great IPA will do the trick. (And here's a suggestion: Take a sip of IPA first and register how it tastes. Then take a bite of cake. Then another sip of beer. The beer and cake together will take on a whole new life....)

Let the mixture cool.

4. Using a rubber spatula, fold the egg whites and whipped cream into the yolks until the mixture is well combined and evenly colored. Fold in the mango purée. Put the semifreddo mixture in a loaf pan or square casserole dish and place in the freezer for a minimum of 4 hours or overnight. When ready to serve, take out of the freezer and let stand for a couple of minutes before slicing.

5. Preheat oven to 375°F.

6. Make the cake: In a large bowl, sift flour and combine with baking powder, sugar, cinnamon, orange zest, orange juice, eggs, and milk. Stir together until smooth. (The mixture should be thick but not doughy. Add some beer a little at a time if you need to loosen the batter.)

7. Butter or grease and lightly flour a 9-inch round baking pan, pour in cake batter, and smooth the top. Bake for 35 to 40 minutes, or until a toothpick inserted in the middle comes out clean.

8. Make the syrup: Combine all the syrup ingredients and heat in a pan over medium-high heat until slightly thickened, about 3 to 5 minutes. Let the syrup cool before you pour over cake.

9. Let cake cool for 20 to 30 minutes, remove from the pan, and place on a plate. Poke many holes in the cake with a wooden skewer or gently poke with a fork. Slowly pour the syrup over the top, allowing it to soak into the cake.

10. Slice the cake, lay a slice of semifreddo on the side, and garnish with diced mangoes and strawberries.

"Sweet and savory together, that's one of my favorite recipe strategies," says Colby Chandler. "Here, I'm using ingredients that echo the main flavor components of a Black Marlin Porter I did with cocoa nibs, chipotle, and orange peel."

CHOCOLATE AND GOAT CHEESE
WITH A BALSAMIC BLACK MARLIN REDUCTION

COLBY CHANDLER, SPECIALTY BREWER, BALLAST POINT BREWING & SPIRITS   *[serves 8]*

Chef's Note: *Any malty dark beer will work great in this recipe. You could also substitute Ballast Point's Sea Monster Imperial Stout for the Black Marlin Porter. To make the infused beer, put 6 cups of beer in a saucepan and cook with ¼ cup of cocoa nibs, a chipotle pepper, and ⅛ cup of orange peel until reduced by a third (to 4 cups).*

4 cups Ballast Point Black Marlin Porter with cocoa nibs, chipotle, and orange peel
2 cups balsamic vinegar
4 ounces 60 percent cacao premium chocolate bar

2 tablespoons raw sugar
1 tablespoon smoked paprika
2 ounces goat cheese, room temperature
1 orange, zested

Job well done! Trenchermen (from left): Colby Chandler, Tyson Blake with son Max, Brandon Brooks, Nate Soroko, Mark Bolton, and Brandon Hernández (supine). Not pictured: Colin Murray

Colby's preference is to pair this recipe with **BALLAST POINT'S BLACK MARLIN PORTER** infused with cocoa nibs, chipotle peppers, and orange peel. If you don't have access to this beer, however, you can easily substitute another chile-infused or chocolately porter, or infuse your own porter.

PERFECT PAIRING

[PREPARATION]

1. In a medium stockpot over medium heat, bring the beer and balsamic vinegar to a boil. Reduce the heat to medium-low and cook until the mixture has reduced by 75 percent. The sauce should be thick and sticky. Reduce heat to low and keep warm.
2. Use a razor or sharp knife to score the smooth side of the chocolate bar into 8 pieces. Break the chocolate at the score marks.
3. Combine the sugar and paprika in a bowl and set aside.
4. Put goat cheese into a piping bag fitted with a star tip.
5. To serve, place a piece of chocolate on each small plate and pipe the goat cheese onto each chocolate piece. Drizzle with the beer reduction. Garnish with a pinch of the sugar mixture and orange zest, and serve.

breakfast | desserts

OATMEAL STOUT-AND-BACON BELGIAN WAFFLES

ERRIN LOVE, CO-OWNER, MOTHER EARTH BREW CO.,
AND JOELLE KHANNAKHJAVANI, TASTING ROOM MANAGER   *[serves 2]*

"*I really love the combination of malty flavors with the flavors of chocolate and coffee,*" *says Kamron Khannakhjavani (pictured with wife, Joelle), co-founder and brewer at Mother Earth. "These are the same flavors I love in a great breakfast—especially in waffles or pancakes." So, what better way to highlight the rich, comforting flavors of Mother Earth's Chocolate Oatmeal Stout than to make it part of a waffle batter? The addition of bacon crumbles adds extra notes of sweetness and saltiness that harmonize perfectly with the beer.*

For the waffles:
2 cups oat flour
3 teaspoons baking powder
½ teaspoon salt
1 teaspoon orange peel
2 eggs
¼ cup oil
1½ cups Mother Earth
    Round About Chocolate
    Oatmeal Stout
1 teaspoon pure vanilla extract
½ cup bacon, cooked crisp and
    crumbled

Finishing touches:
Melted butter
Maple syrup
Powdered sugar
Extra slices crisp bacon

[PREPARATION]
1. Preheat and grease a Belgian waffle iron.
2. In a mixing bowl, combine the flour, baking powder, salt, and orange peel.
3. Add the eggs, oil, beer, and vanilla, and whisk together with a wire whisk. Fold in the bacon.
4. Pour the batter into the prepared waffle iron and cook to golden brown.
5. Serve with drizzled melted butter and maple syrup. Sprinkle with powdered sugar and extra bacon slices, if desired.

PERFECT PAIRING

Beer for breakfast is not uncommon among the truest of craft beer fans. The most popular choices for breakfasts are the rich and sweetly malty stouts and porters. (Of course, Rogue's famous Voodoo Donut has bacon and maple syrup in it, so it's a breakfast beer in the truest sense of the word!)

Rachel King: *"I don't usually use beer in my recipes, but I found that the beer adds a really nice texture to these. The carbonation actually helps in the baking process and creates a delicious, tender crumb."*

SEARSUCKER'S APPLE & ALE MUFFINS

RACHEL KING, PASTRY CHEF, FABRIC OF SOCIAL DINING GROUP   *[makes 12 muffins]*

½ cup plus 3 tablespoons butter
3 apples, peeled, cored, and cut
   into medium dice (I like Granny
   Smith, but Galas or Fujis would
   also work well)
1 cup brown sugar
1 egg

1½ cups all-purpose flour
1 teaspoon baking powder
½ teaspoon baking soda
½ teaspoon ground cinnamon
Pinch salt
1 cup malty beer (my favorite is
   AleSmith's Nautical Nut Brown)

[PREPARATION]

1. Preheat oven to 325°F. Line muffin pans with paper cups or grease them.

2. In a large sauté pan, melt 3 tablespoons of the butter and sauté the apples until soft (about 10 to 15 minutes). Set aside.

3. In a mixing bowl, cream together the remaining butter and brown sugar until fluffy. Add the egg and beat until combined.

4. In a medium bowl, whisk the dry ingredients together. Add the dry mixture to the butter mixture and mix until there are no lumps and everything is incorporated. Stir in the beer and fold in the apples. Fill muffin tins about three-quarters of the way and bake for about 15 minutes. Test for doneness by poking a toothpick in the center of a muffin — the toothpick should come out with just a few crumbs attached. Cool completely before serving.

Who doesn't want more ways to get beer into breakfast? Rachel King, the talented and prolific pastry chef for Searsucker and the other great Brian Malarkey restaurants in the Fabric of Social Dining Group, created this recipe specifically for this book. Rachel says that Searsucker offers a pastry basket for brunch every weekend, so these muffins will likely find their way onto the menu at some point. "I'm really happy with how these turned out."

Rachel says that a malt-forward, low-hop beer is best for making the muffins as well as for pairing. **ALESMITH'S NAUTICAL NUT BROWN** is a particular favorite, but **NEW ENGLISH'S BREWERS SPECIAL BROWN** or **MANZANITA'S GILLESPIE BROWN** are other great choices.

PERFECT PAIRING

NAVIGATOR DOPPLEBOCK BREAD PUDDING
WITH RUM RAISIN CARAMEL AND BLUE CHEESE WHIPPED CREAM

TYSON BLAKE, GENERAL MANAGER, O'BRIEN'S PUB

[serves 10]

This is a dessert that is quite simple to make — it combines a bunch of small, easy steps to create one impressive and very delicious dish. Tyson (above right with O'Brien's owner Tom Nickel) pairs malty flavors from the Dopplebock with rum to prove what a lot of San Diego brewers already know: rich, malty beers become incredible when aged in bourbon, rum, brandy, or whiskey barrels.

For the bread pudding:
1½ cups heavy whipping cream
1 cup Ballast Point Navigator Dopplebock (or other malt-forward beer)
1 cup milk
1 vanilla bean, cut in half lengthwise
1 cup granulated sugar
4 large eggs
3 large egg yolks
½ teaspoon salt
1 tablespoon ground cinnamon
2 teaspoons ginger powder
1 loaf Italian bread, cut into 1-inch cubes and toasted lightly

For the whipped cream:
2 cups heavy whipping cream

¾ cup good-quality blue cheese, crumbled
2 tablespoons powdered sugar

For the rum sauce:
¾ cup dark rum (Ballast Point Three Sheets Rum is awesome!)
1 cup raisins
2 cups granulated sugar
1 cup brown sugar
¾ cup Ballast Point Navigator Dopplebock
¼ cup unsalted butter, softened
¼ cup heavy whipping cream, cold

Finishing touch:
Blue cheese crumbles, optional

[PREPARATION]

1. Make the bread pudding: Preheat oven to 375°F. In a saucepan over medium heat, whisk together the cream, beer, milk, vanilla bean, and ½ cup of the sugar.

continued >

PERFECT PAIRING

If you're a traditionalist, you'll love pairing this dessert with a Dopplebock or even a rich, malty vanilla-infused stout or porter. If you want your mind blown, try pairing it with **BALLAST POINT'S SCULPIN IPA, STONE'S ARROGANT BASTARD, GREEN FLASH'S IMPERIAL IPA**, or some other hoppy IPA. The bitter hops set off the sweetness of the rum sauce and whipped cream perfectly!

Cook until the sugar has dissolved. Remove from the heat and let cool.

2. In a mixing bowl, whisk together the eggs, egg yolks, salt, cinnamon, ginger, and the remaining ½ cup of sugar until all of the ingredients are completely incorporated. While whisking, add a bit of the warm cream-and-beer mixture to the egg mixture and combine well. Still whisking, add the rest of the cream-and-beer mixture to the egg mixture.

3. Add the bread to the liquid, submerging it so it gets completely soaked. Lightly butter a 9-by-13-inch baking dish. Pour the mixture into the baking dish and distribute the bread into an even layer.

4. Bake, uncovered, until the pudding is puffed and set, about 45 minutes.

5. Make the whipped cream: In a saucepan over medium heat, warm 1 cup of the cream and the blue cheese, stirring constantly, for 3 to 5 minutes. Refrigerate and let the mixture cool completely.

6. Whip the remaining 1 cup of cream and powdered sugar until stiff peaks form. Gently fold in the cooled blue cheese cream and chill until ready to serve.

7. Make the rum sauce: In a medium saucepan, heat the rum. Place the raisins in a bowl and cover with the warm rum. Set aside and allow the raisins to plump for about 20 minutes.

8. In a saucepan over medium heat, whisk the sugars and beer. Bring the mixture to a boil, reduce to a simmer, and cook until dark and thick, 10 to 15 minutes.

9. Whisk in the butter until it is completely incorporated. Remove from the heat and stir in the cream. Stir in the raisins and set aside.

10. To serve, cut out a square of the bread pudding and place it on a plate. Drizzle as much rum raisin sauce as you like and spoon on a dollop of whipped cream. Garnish with mint and serve immediately.

GRAND CRU STRAWBERRY AND KUMQUAT GALETTE

KAITLIN JAIME AND MISTY BIRCHALL, PUBCAKES   *[serves 4]*

"This recipe features my grandmother's famous crust," announces PubCakes pastry chef Kaitlin Jaime (left, with Misty Birchall). "It is so buttery and flaky and delicious, it's the best." The original crust was used for pies, but Kaitlin liked the idea of making individual desserts with it. "I just thought it would be more fun, and cute. Plus, you don't need to do them in a pan." What you wind up with, as Kaitlin says, is "a very simple recipe that's very fancy-looking."

For the filling:
1 pint (about 2 cups) kumquats
½ cup plus 2 tablespoons
    granulated sugar
½ cup AleSmith Grand Cru
2 pints (about 4 cups)
    strawberries, hulled and halved
2 tablespoons all-purpose flour

For the crust:
2¼ cups all-purpose flour, sifted
    and refrigerated

2 tablespoons fresh thyme,
    chopped
1 teaspoon salt
¼ cup cold water
½ cup (generously filled)
    vegetable shortening
½ cup unsalted butter, near
    room temperature
1 egg
1 tablespoon water
Raw sugar

[PREPARATION]

1. Make the filling: Add the kumquats to a small saucepan and cover with cold water. Bring the water to a boil and then strain the kumquats and return them to the pan. Repeat this process three times, making sure to use cold water each time. This is an important step, because without it your kumquats will taste bitter in the final dessert.

2. Refrigerate the strained kumquats until cool enough to handle. Once cool, slice the kumquats in half lengthwise and remove the seeds using a small paring knife or your fingers.

3. Return the kumquats to the small saucepan and **continued >**

PERFECT PAIRING

"ALESMITH'S GRAND CRU is very bright and citrusy," Kaitlin says. "It's as bubbly as champagne with an enjoyable yeastiness. We felt that pairing it with strawberries and kumquats would be ideal."

add ½ cup sugar and the AleSmith Grand Cru. Bring to a boil over medium heat until the sugar is dissolved and the mixture has the consistency of a thin syrup.

4. In a bowl, toss the strawberries in the remaining 2 tablespoons of sugar and the flour. Once the strawberries are coated with sugar, add the kumquats and syrup and stir until thoroughly combined.

5. Make the crust: Preheat oven to 350°F. Mix ⅓ cup of the flour with the thyme, salt, and water to create a paste Set aside.

6. In a separate bowl, combine the remaining flour, shortening, and butter. Add the paste to the flour mixture and work with your hands to form a fairly smooth ball.

7. Divide the dough into 4 discs and roll out on a floured surface until each one is ¼ inch thick and about 6 inches in diameter. Transfer to a parchment-lined baking sheet. Add about ½ cup of fruit filling to the center of each round and gently fold over the edges of the crust to create a crater to hold the filling.

8. Whisk egg and water together to create an egg wash. Using a pastry brush, paint the wash onto the crusts and sprinkle with raw sugar.

9. Bake for about 20 minutes, or until the crust is golden brown. Serve with mascarpone cheese, whipped cream, or even some homemade ice cream. And, of course, AleSmith Grand Cru!

TORONADO'S STOUT NUTELLA TRIFLE

NATE SOROKO, HEAD CHEF, TORONADO SAN DIEGO   *[serves 8]*

Chef's Note: *This recipe is best made a day ahead to allow the trifle mixture to chill and solidify. Then chill the assembled trifle for a minumum of 1 hour before serving.*

14 ounces cream cheese
16 ounces nutella
4 pints whipping cream
Granulated sugar, to taste
1 (750-ml) bottle AleSmith

Speedway Stout (or other great coffee-infused stout)
36 ladyfingers
Mixed chocolate grated or shaved, for garnish

[PREPARATION]

1. In a stand mixer, whip the cream cheese and nutella together until smooth. Set aside.

2. In a separate bowl, whisk the whipping cream until it holds stiff peaks. Sweeten to taste.

3. Gently fold the whipped cream into the cream cheese-nutella mixture (try to preserve as much air as possible) and refrigerate for a minimum of 12 hours.

4. In a small pot, gently heat about ¾ cup of stout to a simmer. Turn off heat. In a large trifle bowl, make a layer of ladyfingers and brush them liberally with stout.

5. Spoon or pipe a layer of mousse on top. Add another layer of ladyfingers, brush them with stout (drink the rest!), and top with remaining mousse. Shave chocolate over the top, and refrigerate for a minimum 1 hour before serving.

Nate Soroko (left, with Toronado owner Ian Black) is San Diego's master of the simple-but-incredibly-delicious recipe. "I've always been a fan of Nutella, and I had a recipe for a peanut butter mousse," Nate recalls. "So, I basically just switched the peanut butter out for Nutella." The recipe evolved into something layered with cake, Nate says, "and then a friend of mine said this would be good as a trifle, and — bang! — I thought: Soak the cake in Speedway."

Nate says **SPEEDWAY STOUT** pairs wonderfully with this dessert, but he adds, "You could do any stout — even go and pair with a framboise or just about any great dessert beer or wine."

PERFECT PAIRING

CHOCOLATE AND STOUT POT DE CRÈME
WITH MALT FLORENTINE COOKIES

KATHERINE HUMPHUS, EXECUTIVE CHEF, BO-BEAU KITCHEN + BAR   *[serves 6–8]*

Katherine Humphus is one of San Diego's youngest executive chefs, and there's a reason for that: She's incredibly talented and has a great ability to create food that is comforting and interesting at the same time. "We have pot de crème on our regular menu," Katherine says, "and we're kind of known for doing all sorts of different things with it. Pot de crème is kind of a blank canvas that can work with a wide variety of flavorings. I knew I wanted to do a beer-inspired version, so I created one for this book."

For the pot de crème:
1 cup whole milk
1 cup heavy cream
¼ cup granulated sugar
5 egg yolks
13 ounces bittersweet
   chocolate
3 tablespoons AleSmith
   Speedway Stout

For the cookies:
1½ cups sliced almonds
3 tablespoons brewer's malt
3 tablespoons all-purpose flour
¼ teaspoon salt
¾ cup granulated sugar
2 tablespoons heavy cream
2 tablespoons light corn syrup
5 tablespoons unsalted butter
1 teaspoon pure vanilla extract

[PREPARATION]
1. Make the pot de crème: In a medium saucepan, combine the milk, cream, and sugar. Heat, stirring, until the mixture is hot but not boiling.
2. Place the egg yolks into a large bowl and begin whisking. Slowly pour a little bit of the hot cream mixture into the yolks while continuing to whisk vigorously. Slowly add the remaining cream mixture, whisking continuously to keep the eggs from getting too hot and forming lumps.
3. Return the custard to the saucepan and heat on medium-low heat, stirring constantly, to thicken. The custard is done when it coats the back of a spoon. Remove from heat.
4. Put the chocolate into a bowl. Pour the custard through a fine-mesh

continued >

PERFECT PAIRING

As Chef Katherine says, "**ALESMITH'S SPEEDWAY STOUT** is real dark and chocolately and espresso-like, which is a no-brainer for a pot de crème. It just goes so perfectly."

sieve into the bowl of chocolate. Let sit for 1 minute.

5. Stir to combine the chocolate and custard. Once the chocolate is melted, it's best to use an immersion blender to smooth out the mixture.

6. Add the AleSmith Speedway Stout and combine well.

7. Pour into ramekins or a serving bowl and refrigerate until firm.

8. Make the cookies: Preheat oven to 350°F. Cover a baking sheet with a silicone liner or parchment paper.

9. In a large bowl, stir together the nuts, malt, flour, and salt.

10. In a small saucepan, combine the sugar, cream, corn syrup, and butter. Cook over medium heat, stirring occasionally, until mixture comes to a rolling boil. Continue to boil for 1 minute. Remove from heat and stir in the vanilla.

11. Pour the cream mixture into the dry almond mixture and stir just to combine. Set aside for about 30 minutes until cool enough to handle.

12. Using a small cookie scoop, make little balls and place on prepared baking sheet. Leave plenty of space between cookies, since they will spread quite a bit.

13. Bake for about 10 minutes, or until the cookies are thin and golden brown all around. Cool for 2 minutes on baking sheet, then transfer to a rack to finish cooling.

14. Serve pot de crème with the cookies.

BLACK MARLIN CAKE
WITH COCOA MALT ICE CREAM AND RASPBERRY COULIS

MISTY BIRCHALL, OWNER AND FOUNDER, PUBCAKES

[serves 6–12]

PubCakes founder Misty Birchall (right) explains that she and pastry chef Kaitlin Jaime "wanted to break out of the whole cupcake realm but still make a cupcake. We thought it would be fun to make ice cream and serve it as a component instead of frosting." What they came up with was a fabulous dessert that uses beer in both the cake and the ice cream. "We also added the raspberry coulis as a final touch," Misty says. "It sounds fancy, but it's really easy."

For the ice cream:
6 egg yolks
¾ cup granulated sugar, divided use
1½ cups whole milk
½ cup heavy cream
¼ cup malted milk powder
1 cup Ballast Point Black Marlin Porter
¼ cup bittersweet chocolate chunks

For the cake:
1½ cups all-purpose flour
1 teaspoon baking powder
½ teaspoon baking soda
¼ teaspoon salt

½ cup butter, softened
1 cup brown sugar, packed
1 egg
1 tablespoon pure vanilla extract
1 cup Ballast Point Black Marlin

For the coulis:
2 cups fresh raspberries
2 tablespoon lemon juice
½ cup granulated sugar

Finishing touches:
Chocolate sauce
Whipped cream

[PREPARATION]
1. Make the ice cream: Combine egg yolks with ¼ cup of sugar in a heatproof bowl and whisk until pale yellow. In a saucepan, combine milk, heavy cream, another ¼ cup of the sugar, and malted milk powder. Stir and heat until scalding hot (be careful not to boil). Remove from heat.
2. Temper the egg yolks by gradually adding about one-third of the hot

continued >

PERFECT PAIRING

Misty says **BALLAST POINT'S BLACK MARLIN** was the inspiration for this recipe. "We wanted to make a malted ice cream and pair it with a malty porter because this ingredient is common in brewing and desserts," she says. "I think people tend to forget that." For pairing, a great porter or stout with rich maltiness and chocolate flavors will surely please.

milk mixture at a time, whisking constantly. Return the tempered egg mixture to the saucepan and cook on low heat, stirring constantly, until just thick enough to coat the back of a spoon.

3. Fill a large bowl with ice and water to create an ice bath. Remove the saucepan from the heat and strain the custard into a metal bowl. Immediately place the metal bowl in the ice bath. Cool the custard to below 40°F, cover, and refrigerate for a minimum of 12 hours, or overnight. At this time, you should also put your ice cream maker bowl into the freezer.

4. Combine the beer and the remaining ¼ cup of sugar in a saucepan and heat over low heat, swirling occasionally, until reduced to ¼ cup. Pour into a heatproof container and cool to room temperature.

5. Process the cream mixture in an ice cream maker according to the manufacturer's instructions. When the ice cream is done, add the beer reduction and bittersweet chocolate chunks and mix in well. Freeze in containers for several hours or overnight.

6. Preheat oven to 350°F. Line the wells of a cupcake pan with paper liners.

7. Make the cake: In a medium bowl, sift together the dry ingredients. Set aside.

8. In a large mixing bowl, cream the butter and brown sugar on high until the mixture lightens and increases in volume. Add the egg and vanilla, and beat in well.

9. Set the mixer to low and add dry ingredients and beer, alternating in one-third increments, until fully incorporated.

10. Using an ice cream scoop or large spoon, fill the cupcake liners about three-quarters full. Bake for about 15 minutes, rotating the pan in the oven half way through the cooking time for even baking. The cupcakes are done when a skewer inserted into the center comes out clean. Remove cupcakes from the pan as soon as they are cool enough to touch. (This will prevent the bottoms from steaming.)

11. Make the coulis: Combine all ingredients in a saucepan and heat on medium heat, stirring periodically, until the raspberries break down and the sauce thickens enough to coat the back of a spoon.

12. Assemble the cupcakes: Remove cupcake liners from cupcakes and top each with a scoop of ice cream and a drizzle of raspberry coulis.

ROCK BOTTOM STOUT CUPCAKES

RECIPE BY ROCK BOTTOM DREWERY, GASLAMP QUARTER, SAN DIEGO   *[makes 18 cupcakes]*

Rock Bottom's chef, Jeff Logsdon (left, with Brewmaster Jason Stockberger), knows what most dessert-loving beer fans know: Chocolate baked goods and porters and stouts are made to go together. "It's a classic pairing that really brings out the best aspects of the food as well as the beer," Jeff says. The most critical step in this recipe is allowing the batter to rest before putting it in the oven. "That allows all the air pockets to collapse and gives you a more evenly baked cake."

For the batter:
4 cups stout or porter, measured
   without foam
4 sticks (2 cups) butter, melted
1½ cups unsweetened cocoa
   powder
4 cups all-purpose flour
3½ cups granulated sugar
3 teaspoons baking soda
1½ teaspoons salt
8 ounces sour cream
4 eggs

For the frosting:
3 sticks (1½ cups) butter,
   softened
24 ounces cream cheese,
   softened
16 ounces powdered sugar
1½ teaspoons pure vanilla
   extract

Finishing touches:
Caramel sauce
Chocolate or fudge sauce

[PREPARATION]
1. Preheat oven to 375°F.
2. In a sauté pan, heat the beer until reduced by half. Add the butter and stir to combine.
3. In the bowl of a mixer, combine the cocoa powder, flour, sugar, baking soda, and salt. Mix on low for 1 minute, or until well combined.
4. Slowly add the beer mixture to the dry ingredients, and mix until well incorporated.
5. Add the sour cream and mix. Add the eggs and mix on medium speed

continued >

PERFECT PAIRING

Rock Bottom's award-winning brewer, Jason Stockberger, has a special love for the stouts and porters he makes. "They are usually my favorites," Jason admits — though he's quick to say that he loves ALL the beer he makes! "A really great chocolate cake paired with a malty, chocolately beer with vanilla and coffee notes…that's my idea of perfection."

until smooth.

6. Allow the batter to rest for 20 minutes (to remove air pockets).

7. Place paper liners in the wells of muffin pans or grease the wells. Fill liners with equal amounts of batter and place in the oven for 20 to 25 minutes. Insert a skewer into the middle of a cupcake after 20 minutes. If the skewer comes out clean, the cupcakes are done. Cool at room temperature.

8. Make the frosting: In a mixer with a paddle attachment, whip the butter until it becomes light in color and doubles in volume (approximately 5 minutes).

9. Add the cream cheese and whip for 2 minutes. Scrape down the sides of the bowl.

10. Add the powdered sugar and vanilla, and mix on low speed until smooth and creamy (approximately 2 minutes). Refrigerate until needed.

11. Frost cupcakes and drizzle with caramel sauce and/or hot fudge sauce. Serve.

HIGH DIVE WAHOO LEMON BARS

INGRID QUA, OWNER, HIGH DIVE BAR

[makes about 12 bars]

For the crust:
½ cup granulated sugar
1 cup butter, softened
¼ cup Ballast Point Wahoo Wheat
2 cups all-purpose flour

For the filling:
4 eggs
¼ cup all-purpose flour

4 lemons, juiced
½ cup Ballast Point Wahoo Wheat
2 tablespoons Ballast Point White Rum
1½ cups granulated sugar

Finishing touch:
Powdered sugar, optional

[PREPARATION]

1. Make the crust: Preheat oven to 350°F. In a bowl, combine the sugar, butter, beer, and flour. Mix well to incorporate the ingredients evenly.

2. Press the dough evenly into an ungreased 13-by-9-inch pan. (You can use the bottom of a glass to press the dough and to make sure you get equal thickness throughout the pan.)

3. Bake for 25 minutes, or until the crust firms up and browns slightly. (It's important that the crust be a golden brown and just starting to crisp so it has the structure to hold the filling.)

4. Make the filling: Place the filling ingredients in a bowl and whisk to combine well. Pour the filling over the crust and bake for another 20 minutes.

5. Remove from oven and let stand until cool and firm. It is best to refrigerate overnight and bring back to room temperature before serving. Sprinkle with powdered sugar, if desired.

Ingrid loves pairing these bars with **CORONADO'S IDIOT IPA** because it has such strong citrus character. Other citrus-forward IPAs, such as **BALLAST POINT'S SCULPIN**, **ALPINE'S NELSON** or **PURE HOPPINESS**, **SOCIETE'S PUPIL IPA**, and **GREEN FLASH'S WEST COAST** or **IMPERIAL IPA**, would work well too.

PERFECT PAIRING

"I am a huge lemon bar fanatic," Ingrid Qua admits with a shy smile. "I live and breathe lemon bars." She also admits that, until recently, she had never baked anything. So, when she decided to try her hand in the kitchen, she set her sights on the thing she loves most: lemon bars. Her newfound talent comes in handy when she talks to women about trying IPAs. "I always tell them to try it with a lemon bar."

OLDER VISCOSITY STOUT CAKE
WITH WHIPPED CREAM AND GANACHE GLAZE

SEAN KENNEDY, LEAD BARTENDER, PORT BREWING AND THE LOST ABBEY   *[serves 12]*

"Most recipes you find for stout cakes recommend beers that are light and relatively flavorless," says Sean Kennedy, lead bartender at Port Brewing and The Lost Abbey. "So, I wanted to make a cake that had nice, big, complex tastes." Sean says that to him, the perfect dessert is one where you take a first bite and get some delicious flavors, but then as you dig into it, "you get more and more flavors coming into play."

For the cake:
1 cup unsalted butter, plus more for cake pan
1 cup Port Brewing Older Viscosity Stout
¾ cup unsweetened cocoa powder
2 cups all-purpose flour
2 cups granulated sugar
1½ teaspoons baking soda
¾ teaspoon salt
2 large eggs
⅔ cup sour cream

For the ganache glaze:
6 ounces semisweet chocolate chips (I like Ghirardelli)
6 tablespoons heavy cream
¾ teaspoon instant coffee (I like Starbucks Via)

For the whipped cream:
2 cups heavy whipping cream
1 teaspoon pure vanilla extract
1 teaspoon almond extract
2 tablespoons granulated sugar

[PREPARATION]
1. Prepare the cake batter: Preheat oven to 350°F. Butter or oil a Bundt pan. In a medium saucepan, heat the butter and the beer to a simmer over medium heat. Remove from heat and whisk in the cocoa powder. Set aside.
2. In a medium bowl, thoroughly combine flour, sugar, baking soda, and salt.
3. In another bowl, beat the eggs and the sour cream together until

continued >

PERFECT PAIRING

Needless to say, this cake pairs beautifully with **PORT BREWING'S OLDER VISCOSITY**, which has big notes of vanilla and malt, along with subtle notes of coconut. Other great choices: **LOST ABBEY'S SERPENT STOUT**, which has big coffee and chocolate notes; **GREEN FLASH'S SILVA STOUT** or **DOUBLE STOUT**.

Sean's special tip for making this cake a success is "quality ingredients. Use the best chocolate, cocoa powder, and stout you can find."

well-blended. Stir the egg and sour cream mixture into the stout mixture until just blended. Add the wet ingredients to the dry ingredients in two or three batches, mixing after each addition with an electric mixer.

4. Pour the batter into the Bundt pan and bake for 35 minutes, or until a toothpick inserted in the middle of the cake comes out clean. Cool on a rack completely before inverting the pan to release the cake.

5. Make the glaze: In the top of a double boiler set over simmering water, gently stir together the chocolate, heavy cream, and coffee until melted. Remove from heat and allow a few minutes to cool and thicken. Pour over the cake.

6. Make the whipped cream: Combine all ingredients in a mixing bowl and whip to medium peaks. Serve alongside a slice of cake and a glass of great stout or porter.

MOTHER EARTH MANCAKES
WITH VANILLA CREAM ALE FROSTING

JOELLE KHANNAKHJAVANI, RETAIL SALES MANAGER, MOTHER EARTH BREW CO. *[makes about 24 cupcakes]*

For the batter:
1 box of your favorite chocolate
   cake mix (preferably dark
   chocolate or double chocolate)
1 cup mayonnaise
3 eggs
1½ cups Mother Earth Night Shift
   Coffee Porter (or other great
   coffee porter)

For the frosting:
½ cup softened butter
1 teaspoon pure vanilla extract
⅓ cup Mother Earth Cali Creamin'
   Vanilla Cream Ale
3½ cups powdered sugar

Finishing touches:
Coffee beans, mint leaves

[PREPARATION]
1. Make the batter: Preheat the oven according to the cake-mix directions. In a medium-large bowl, combine the dry cake mix with the mayonnaise, eggs, and beer. (You can add more beer to taste, as long as the batter doesn't get runny.)
2. Pour the batter into a nonstick or greased cupcake pan and bake as directed on the cake mix. Remove from the oven and allow to cool completely before frosting.
3. Make the frosting: In a bowl, combine the butter, vanilla, and beer, mixing on low. Slowly incorporate the powdered sugar, mixing on medium until the frosting is thick.
4. Frost the cupcakes and enjoy a little bit of heaven with Mother Earth!

"I originally made these for my brother's engagement party," explains Joelle. *"My brother and his fiancée really love beer, and my brother's favorite flavor is chocolate, so I knew I wanted to use a dark, roasty, malty porter in the batter."* Quick, easy, and open to variations and experimentation, this recipe is a great option for a beer-centric dessert that will please a crowd but not take hours to prepare.

MOTHER EARTH'S NIGHT SHIFT PORTER is a rich, malty, chocolately porter that's bursting with coffee flavor. It's the ideal beer to pair with this dessert, but any great porter or stout (with or without notes of coffee) will work beautifully.

PERFECT PAIRING

NO JUDGMENT HERE GOAT CHEESE AND RASPBERRY CHEESECAKE
WITH BEER CARAMEL AND FRESH BERRIES

BRANDON BROOKS, EXECUTIVE CHEF, SOL MARKETS   *[serves 12]*

SOL Market is one of San Diego's newest enterprises, dedicated to providing local produce, food, and beverages of the highest quality. In keeping with the market's mission, Executive Chef Brandon Brooks creates his dishes with the freshest local ingredients, and this cheesecake is simple to make and very impressive when it's done.

For the crust:
1 cup all-purpose flour
½ cup powdered sugar
½ cup cold butter, cubed
1 teaspoon pure vanilla extract

For the filling:
375 milliliters (½ bottle) Lost Abbey Judgment Day
1½ cups granulated sugar
2 pounds chevre (goat cheese), room temperature

5 eggs
½ pint fresh raspberries

For the caramel:
375 milliliters (½ bottle) Judgment Day
1 cup granulated sugar
2 tablespoons butter

Finishing touches:
Fresh berries, optional
Fresh mint, optional

[PREPARATION]
1. Preheat oven to 375°F.
2. Make the crust: In a medium bowl, combine all the crust ingredients and work them with your hands until they come together to form a smooth and consistent dough.
3. Press the dough into a 9-inch round baking dish, forming an even layer, and bake for 15 minutes. Crust should be a light golden brown. Set aside to cool.

continued >

PERFECT PAIRING

JUDGMENT DAY is a massive Belgian dark quad-style ale. It's thick, rich, and malty with full flavors of chocolate and caramel. The Belgian yeastiness in this beer pairs particularly well with the goat cheese. Although it's tough to come up with lots of comparable beers, you could pair this dessert with any great quad-style beer or malty, caramel-laden trippel.

Brandon Brooks: "This cheesecake is an awesome recipe, made even better by fresh local goat cheese and the freshest, most delicious raspberries." Brandon explains that he also designed the recipe to use local beer, but "Lost Abbey's Judgment Day is so good, I'd probably use it no matter where we were."

4. Make the filling: In a medium saucepan over medium heat, combine the beer and sugar. Cook until a thick syrup has formed (10 to 12 minutes).

5. In a bowl, combine the reduced beer and sugar mixture with the goat cheese and whisk until thoroughly combined. Add eggs and whisk until all the ingredients have come together. Gently fold in the raspberries with a spoon or spatula.

6. Pour the filling onto the crust and set the baking pan into a larger baking dish. Carefully pour warm water into the larger dish to create a water bath that comes two-thirds of the way up the pan.

7. Bake for 1 hour, or until a skewer or knife inserted into the middle of the cheesecake comes out clean. Refrigerate, uncovered, at least 4 hours, or preferably overnight.

8. Make the caramel: In a small saucepan, combine the beer and sugar and cook on medium to high. Once the mixture is reduced by at least three-quarters, stir in the butter until it dissolves completely. Remove the saucepan from the heat. The caramel may be served warm or cold.

9. Serve wedges of cheesecake drizzled with the caramel, along with berries and mint, if desired.

CHRIS CRAMER'S FAVORITE IMPERIAL STOUT CRÈME BRÛLÉE

RECIPE BY GUNTHER EMATHINGER, EXECUTIVE CHEF,
KARL STRAUSS BREWING COMPANY

[makes 6]

For Chris Cramer, co-founder and co-owner of Karl Strauss Brewing Company, picking his favorite Gunther Emathinger recipe was a snap. "Gunther makes the best crème brûlée in San Diego, hands down," Chris says proudly. "I first had his crème brûlée probably 20 years ago, when he was working as a chef downtown, and, of all the brûlées I've had since, this still holds up as the best."

2 cups Karl Strauss Wreck Alley
   Imperial Stout
4 cups heavy cream
1 vanilla bean

1 cup granulated sugar, plus more
   for topping
12 egg yolks
Fresh banana slices, if desired

[PREPARATION]

1. Preheat oven to 325°F. In a medium pan, bring the stout to a slow boil and cook until reduced to ¼ cup.

2. Place cream in a nonreactive saucepan. Split the vanilla bean lengthwise and scrape the seeds into the cream. (The pod can be used as an additional flavor enhancer by adding it to the cream while heating, but remove it and discard before whisking.)

3. Heat cream and vanilla slowly until steaming. Remove from heat. Do not allow the cream to boil.

4. In a medium bowl, whisk the sugar and egg yolks together with wire whisk until pale in color and sugar is dissolved, about 1 to 2 minutes. Pour about ½ cup of the hot cream into the egg mixture, whisking constantly to prevent the egg from cooking.

5. In a slow stream, add the remaining hot cream to the egg mixture while continuing to stir with the whisk. Add the reduced stout and mix well.

6. Divide the mixture evenly into 6 shallow ovenproof ramekins, and place the ramekins in a deep baking dish. Fill the baking dish with hot water to

continued >

PERFECT PAIRING

Chef Gunther uses **WRECK ALLEY** — Karl's coffee-infused Imperial Stout — to add chocolate, vanilla, malt, and bourbon notes to the dish. For drinking, a rich, creamy porter or stout as an accompaniment to this dessert would be pure heaven…

come halfway up the sides of the ramekins. Cook for 40 minutes, or until just set. (Check for doneness by gently shaking the ramekins; the crème brûlée is done when the edges are set and firm but the middle jiggles a little.) Refrigerate for at least 2 hours to cool before serving.

7. To serve, lay a couple of banana slices on top of each crème brûlée, if desired, then sprinkle a thin layer of granulated sugar. With a kitchen propane torch (available at cookware stores), point the flame onto the sugar and heat until it begins to melt and is a deep golden brown color. (You can also use the broiler setting of your oven to brown the sugar by placing the ramekins about an inch under the broiler for 20 to 30 seconds.) Garnish with sliced strawberries and powdered sugar.

GREEN TEA LAYER CAKE WITH BEER FROSTING TWO WAYS

KAREN BLAIR, HAMILTON'S TAVERN, SMALL BAR, ELEVEN, AND MONKEY PAW BAR PUB & BREWERY

[serves 12]

Hamilton's Tavern is legendary in San Diego for its Second Saturday events, held every month at the bar. Karen Blair develops the recipes from dishes she and her husband make at home, executing them for hundreds of people at a time. "This recipe came about for an Asian-inspired Second Saturday featuring Ballast Point," Karen recalls.

For the cake:
1 cup all-purpose flour
1 cup cake flour (or a total of 2 cups of all-purpose flour only if you don't have cake flour)
1 teaspoon baking soda
1 teaspoon salt
2 cups green tea powder, or as desired (available at Whole Foods)
1¼ cups granulated sugar
1 cup vegetable oil
3 eggs
2 teaspoons pure vanilla extract
1 cup plain yogurt

For the Barmy Ale frosting:
1½ cups powdered sugar
2 tablespoons butter, softened
3 ounces cream cheese, softened
½ teaspoon pure vanilla extract
¼ cup Ballast Point Barmy Ale
Drop of yellow and/or red food coloring, if desired

For the Sour Wench frosting:
1½ cups powdered sugar
2 tablespoons butter, softened
3 ounces cream cheese, softened
½ teaspoon pure vanilla extract
¼ cup Ballast Point Sour Wench (or lambic-style beer)
Drop of red food coloring, if desired

[PREPARATION]
1. Preheat oven to 350°F.
2. Grease and flour 2 (9-inch) round cake pans.
3. Start the batter: Sift together the flours, baking soda, salt, and green tea powder, and set aside.

continued >

PERFECT PAIRING

Pairing a beer with cake can be a challenge, especially because there are numerous contrasting flavors happening within the cake itself. Best recommendation: Experiment. If you want to add sweetness, pair with a stout, porter, or even a Belgian quad. If you want to cut sweetness, try a pale ale or even a hefeweizen.

Karen Blair: "I try to incorporate rare or specialty beers we have on draught for our events to make my dishes stand out. These two special ales added to the frosting made this dessert really sing."

4. In a large bowl, whisk sugar, oil, and eggs until smooth. Add vanilla. Slowly whisk in a little of the flour mixture, alternating with some of the yogurt and mixing just until all is incorporated. Pour into prepared pans.

5. Bake for 30 to 40 minutes, or until a toothpick inserted into the center of the cake comes out clean. Cool on wire rack for 30 minutes before turning out of the pans.

6. Make the frostings: For each frosting, combine all ingredients in a mixing bowl and beat with a hand mixer until smooth. Add more powdered sugar if needed to sweeten or thicken the frosting.

7. Assemble the cakes: When the cakes are completely cooled, put one layer on a flat serving plate. (If the cake tops are rounded, you may want to slice the tops with a serrated bread knife to flatten them.) Spread an even layer of Sour Wench Frosting over the top of one cake. Place the other layer of cake on top and spread the Barmy Ale Frosting to cover the top and sides of cake. Decorate with bright edible flowers.

Randy Clemens: "When I got big into beer, I started thinking 'wouldn't it be cool to make beer hog somehow?' I searched around online, didn't find anything, so I decided to just start playing with it."

RUSSIAN IMPERIAL BEER NOG

RANDY CLEMENS, MEDIA & COMMUNICATIONS LINCHPIN, STONE BREWING CO. *[makes 8]*

Chef's Notes: *This recipe uses raw eggs. If you're concerned about the risks of salmonella, you can find in-shell pasteurized eggs in most grocery stores. Also, if Port Old Viscosity is not available in your area, other strong, dark beers may be substituted. Avoid drier stouts and anything with a strong hoppy or bitter profile.*

6 eggs, separated
½ cup plus 2 tablespoons granulated sugar
1 teaspoon pure vanilla extract
2½ cups whole milk
1½ cups heavy cream

10 ounces Stone Imperial Russian Stout or Port Brewing Old Viscosity (or other dark, strong ale)
2 teaspoons freshly ground nutmeg, plus more for garnish

[PREPARATION]

1. In the bowl of a stand mixer with the whisk attachment, beat the egg yolks with ½ cup sugar and the vanilla for several minutes, until the yolks lighten in color and double in volume.

2. Lower the speed of the mixer and add milk, cream, beer, and nutmeg, stirring until combined. Pour yolk mixture into another bowl and reserve.

3. Wash mixer bowl and whisk attachment thoroughly. Any traces the yolk mixture left on equipment will keep the egg whites from whipping properly.

4. Place the egg whites in the clean mixer bowl and beat on high. Gradually add the 2 tablespoons of sugar and continue beating until stiff peaks form.

5. Gently fold the whites into the yolk mixture. Chill and serve. Top each glass with additional grated nutmeg, if desired.

"Long ago, I began to wonder about what made eggnog and why it was generally so bad out of a carton," explains Randy Clemens. "I started watching cooking shows and looking at recipes and then made my own eggnog for a holiday party that was a big hit. Homemade nog is so, so different from anything you'll ever get from a carton. This actually tastes like something good."

PERFECT PAIRING

Randy found while developing this recipe that in addition to **STONE'S IMPERIAL RUSSIAN STOUT**, it works great with **PORT BREWING'S OLD VISCOSITY, ALESMITH'S SPEEDWAY STOUT** and **NORTH COAST OLD RASPUTIN**. Randy encourages experimentation with the recipe. It works well with "just about any dark, rich stout," he says.

resources
featured businesses

**AleSmith
Brewing Company**
9368 Cabot Drive
San Diego, CA 92126
(858) 549-9888
www.alesmith.com

Aztec Brewing Company
2330 La Mirada Drive #300
Vista, CA 92081
(760) 598-7720
aztecbrewery.com

Back Street Brewery
15 Main Street #100
Vista, CA 92084
(760) 407-7600
www.lamppostpizza.com

**Ballast Point
Brewing & Spirits**
10051 Old Grove Road
San Diego, CA 92131
(858) 695-2739
www.ballastpoint.com

Blind Lady Ale House
3416 Adams Ave.
San Diego, CA 92116
(619) 255-2491
www.blindladyalehouse.com

Bo-Beau Kitchen + Bar
4996 W. Point Loma Blvd.
San Diego, CA 92107
(619) 224-2884
www.bobeaukitchen.com

Bunz
475 Hotel Circle South
San Diego, CA 92108
(619) 298-6515
bunzsd.com

**Chicks for Beer @
The High Dive**
1801 Morena Blvd.
San Diego, CA 92110
(619) 275-0460
www.highdiveinc.com

Churchill's Pub & Grille
887 W. San Marcos Blvd.
San Marcos, CA 92078
(760) 471-8773
www.churchillspub.us

**Company Pub
and Kitchen**
13670 Poway Road
Poway, CA 92064
(858) 668-3365
companypubandkitchen.com

Gingham
8384 La Mesa Blvd.
La Mesa, CA 91942
(619) 797-1922
www.ginhameats.com

Green Flash Brewing Co.
6550 Mira Mesa Blvd.
San Diego, CA 92121
(858) 622-0085
www.greenflashbrew.com

**The Grill at The Lodge
at Torrey Pines**
11480 North Torrey
Pines Road
La Jolla, CA 92037
(858) 453-4420
www.lodgetorreypines.com

Handlery Hotel, San Diego
950 Hotel Circle North
San Diego, CA 92108
(619) 298-0511
sd.handlery.com

Hamilton's Tavern
1521-30th St.
San Diego, CA 92102
(619) 238-5460
www.hamiltonstavern.com

Hess Brewing
7955 Silverton Ave. #1201
San Diego, CA 92126
(619) 272-9041
www.hessbrewing.com

Home Brew Mart
5401 Linda Vista Road #406
San Diego, CA 92110
(619) 295-2337
www.homebrewmart.com

Iron Fist Brewing Co.
1305 Hot Spring Way #101
Vista, CA 92081
(760) 216-6500
www.ironfistbrewing.com

**Karl Strauss
Brewing Company**
Main Brewery
5985 Santa Fe Street
San Diego, CA 92109
(858) 273-2739
www.karlstrauss.com

Lightning Brewery
13200 Kirkham Way
Poway, CA 92064
(858) 513-8070
www.lightningbrewery.com

Local Habit
3827-5th Ave.
San Diego, CA 92103
(619) 795-4770
www.mylocalhabit.com

Manzanita Brewing Co.
9962 Prospect Ave. #E
Santee, CA 92071
(619) 334-1757
www.manzanitabrewing.com

The Marine Room
2000 Spindrift Drive
La Jolla, CA 92037
(866) 644-2351
www.marineroom.com

MIHO Gastrotruck
mihogastrotruck.com/
info@MIHOgastrotruck.com

Mission Brewery
1441 L St.
San Diego, CA 92101
(619) 544-0555
www.missionbrewery.com

**Monkey Paw
Pub & Brewery**
805-16th St.
San Diego, CA 92101
(619) 358-9901

Mother Earth Brew Co.
2055 Thibodo Road #H
Vista, CA 92081
(760) 599-4225
www.motherearthbrewco.com

New English Brewing Co.
1795 Hancock St.
San Diego, CA 92110
(619) 857-8023
www.newenglishbrewing.com

O'Brien's Pub
4646 Convoy St.
San Diego, CA 92111
(858) 715-1745
www.obrienspub.net

**Port Brewing Company/
The Lost Abbey**
155 Mata Way #104
San Marcos, CA 92069
(800) 918-6816
www.lostabbey.com

PubCakes
7229 El Cajon Blvd.
San Diego, CA 92115
(619) 741-0530
www.pubcakes.com

Ritual Tavern
4095-30th St.
San Diego, CA 92104
(619) 283-1618
www.ritualtavern.com

Riviera Supper Club
7777 University Ave.
La Mesa, CA 91941
(619) 713-6777
www.rivierasupperclub.com

**Rock Bottom Restaurant
& Brewery, Gaslamp**
401 G St.
San Diego, CA 92101
(619) 231-7000
www.rockbottom.com

**San Diego
Brewing Company**
10450 Friars Road #L
San Diego, CA 92120
(619) 284-2739
www.sandiegobrewing.com

Searsucker
611 Fifth Ave.
San Diego, CA 92101
(619) 233-7327
www.searsucker.com

Small Bar
4628 Park Blvd.
San Diego, CA 92116
(619) 795-7998
www.smallbarsd.com

Societe Brewing Company
8262 Clairemont Mesa Blvd.
San Diego, CA 92111
www.societebrewing.com

Sol Markets
2855 Perry Road
San Diego, CA 92106
(619) 795-6000
www.solmarkets.com

Stone Brewing Co.
1999 Citracado Parkway
Escondido, CA 92029
(760) 471-4999
www.stonebrew.com

Taste Cheese
Contact Mary Palmer
tastecheese@yahoo.com
mary@tastecheese.com

Tiger! Tiger!
3025 El Cajon Blvd.
San Diego, CA 92104
(619) 487-0101
www.tigertigertavern.com

Toronado
4026-30th St.
San Diego, CA 92104
(619) 282-0456
www.toronadosd.com

Urban Solace
3823-30th St.
San Diego, CA 92104
(619) 295-6464
www.urbansolace.net

URGE Gastropub
16761 Bernardo Center
Drive
San Diego, CA 92128
(858) 673-8743
www.urgegastropub.com

The Vine Cottage
6062 Lake Murray Blvd.
#101A
La Mesa, CA 91942
(619) 465-0198
www.thevinecottage.com

White Labs
9495 Candida St.
San Diego, CA 92126
(858) 693-3441
www.whitelabs.com

index

Recipes in bold

A

AleSmith Brewing Company, 22, 18, 71

AleSmith's Wee Heavy Artisan Bread, 22-24

Avant-Garde Herb-Crusted Lamb Medallions, 161-163

Aztec Brewing Company, 126

B

Back Street Brewery, 108

Ballast Point Brewing & Spirits, 14, 103, 150, 166, 168, 179

BBQ'd Jerked Barleywine Chicken with Succotash, 136

Beer Bitty, 142

Beer Cheese Soup, 38

Bergman, Kyle, 9, 25, 140

Bernauer, Karen, 30

Birchall, Misty, 9, 188, 194

Black, Ian, 191

Black Marlin Cake, 194

Blake, Tyson, 10, 18, 50–57, 103, 164, 165, 166, 167, 176, 179, 180

Blake, Max, 166, 179

Blair, Karen, 66, 152, 208

Blair, Scot, 66

Blind Lady Ale House, 9, 94

Bo-Beau Kitchen + Bar, 9, 69, 192

Boucheron (cheese), 55, 56

Bolton, Mark, 179

Brewmaster's Beer-Battered Fish Tacos, 78

Brooks, Brandon, 136, 137, 166, 171, 179, 204, 205

Brown Butter-Seared Scallops, 69

Brune, Nick, 82

Bunz Burger with Smoked Porter Bacon Jam, 88

Bunz Gourmet Burgers, 88, 96, 110

Burgers and Dogs Surf & Turf, 44-47

C

Café Chloe, 138

Cali Belgique Braised Pork, 82

Camembert (cheese), 52, 53

Campbell, Mike, 41, 100

Carballo, Alex, 10, 37, 122

Cauliflower, Beer, and Gruyere Soup, 33

Chandler, Colby, 75, 167, 168, 179

Chef Gunther's Pot Roast Sliders, 147

Cherney, Yuseff, 150

Chicks for Beer Chica Fresca Shrimp Ceviche, 29

Chile Wahoo Wheat Mixta Ceviche on Duck-Fat Tortillas, 171

Chocolate and Goat Cheese, 179

Chocolate and Stout Pot de Crème, 192

Chris Cramer's Favorite Imperial Stout Crème Brulee, 206

Chris Gort's Brewer's Flatbread Pizza, 108

Churchill's Pub & Grille, 131, 155

Cinnamon-Dusted Pork Tenderloin, 118-121

Classic San Diego Fish Tacos, 30

Clemens, Randy, 11, 210, 211

Company Pub and Kitchen, 21

Company Pub's Carrot and Orange Soup, 21

Coq au Bier, 140

Cowboy Chicken Sandwich, 110

Crab-Stuffed Wontons, 34

Cramer, Chris, 206

Creole Eggs in Purgatory, 84-87

Crute, Jim, 105, 106

D

Danderand, Jason, 32, 33

E

Easy Aztec Mac & Cheese, 126
Egan, John, 78, 79
Emathinger, Gunther, 10, 145, 147, 158, 206

F

Fabric of Social Dining Group, 185
Faulk, Claudia, 126
Flores, Michael, 156
Freese, Derek, 38, 39
Friedman, Sara, 60, 61

G

Ginger Mussels and Sour Wench, 75
Gingham, 9, 92
Gingham's Beer-Braised Lamb Shanks, 92
Gordon, Matt, 129, 130
Gort, Christopher, 108
Goulash and Dumplings, 150
Graham, Barbara, 14
Green Flash Barleywine-Glazed Salmon, 64
Green Flash Brewing Co., 53, 64
Green, Peter, 20, 21
Green Tea Layer Cake with Beer Frosting Two Ways, 208
Grilled Lamb Chops, 173
Gruyere (cheese), 54
Guillas, Bernard, 63

H

Hamilton's Tavern, 64, 152, 208
Handlery Hotel San Diego, 124
Hefeweizen Coriander-Baked Sea Bass, 76
Hernández, Brandon, 44, 45, 47, 84, 87, 118, 121, 164, 165, 167
Hess Brewing, 80

Hess Brewing's Grazias Para Paella, 80
Hicks, Brian, 66
High Dive Bar, 29, 199
High Dive Wahoo Lemon Bars, 199
Hinkley, Mike, 53
Hopkins, Kevin, 161, 162
Hop Union, 54
Humphus, Katherine, 9, 69, 70, 192

I

Imperial Stout Pot Roast, 155
Iron Fist Brewing Co., 41, 100

J

Jaime, Kaitlin, 188, 194
Judgment Day Steamed Carlsbad Mussels, 63

K

Karl Strauss Brewing Company, 10, 145, 147, 158, 206
Kennedy, Sean, 200, 201
Khannakhjavani, Joelle, 182, 203
Khannakhjavani, Kamron, 182
Kim, Phon, 114
King, Rachel, 9, 184, 185
Koch, Greg, 40, 122
Koch, Irene, 40

L

Lacey, Simon, 156
Lamb, Ryan, 164, 165
LaMonica, Aaron, 9, 94
Lewis, Heather, 142
Liautard, Marc, 9, 113
Lightning Brewery, 105
Lightning Pulled Pork Sandwiches, 105-107
Lil' Devil Salad, 18
Live Wire Bar, 98
Local Habit, 82
Lodge at Torrey Pines (The), 9, 25, 140

Logsdon, Jeff, 196
Long Beans Topped with a Fried Egg, 43
Lost Abbey (The), 33, 161, 200
Love, Errin, 182

M

Malarkey, Brian, 9, 185
Matt Rattner's Favorite BBQ Carnitas Pizza, 158
Manzanita Brewing Co., 34
Marine Room (The), 9, 63, 76
Mays, Tim, 98
McIlheney, Pat, 53
McIntyre, Shane, 116
Mello, Louis, 66
MIHO Gastrotruck, 60
Mimolette (cheese), 49, 50, 51
Miron, Juan, 60
Mission Brewery, 78, 138
Monkey Paw Bar Pub & Brewery, 38, 152
Montgomery Cheddar (cheese), 54, 55
Mother Earth Brew Co., 182, 203
Mother Earth Mancakes, 203
Murray, Colin, 179
Murphy, Brian, 98

N

Navigator Dopplebock Bread Pudding, 186
New English Brewing Co., 140
Nickel, Lindsey, 52, 53
Nickel, Tom, 50–56, 103, 186
No Judgment Here Goat Cheese and Raspberry Cheesecake, 204

O

Oatmeal Stout-and-Bacon Belgian Waffles, 182
O'Brien's Pub, 10, 18, 50, 103, 176, 186
Older Viscosity Stout Cake, 200
Oliver, Ron, 9, 76, 77

Orange Sculpin Cake with Orange-Mango Semifreddo, 176

P

Palmer, Mary, 50-56
Parker, Neva, 43, 114
Parmigiano-Reggiano, 50, 53
Paul Segura's Favorite Big Beer Burger, 145
Pitman, Garry, 34
Port Brewing Company, 161, 200
Prohaska, Karl, 124
PubCakes, 9, 188, 194
Purple Haze (cheese), 54

Q

Qua, Ingrid, 29, 199
Quad-Braised Osso Buco, 142

R

Ramirez, Adrian, 10, 156
Ratliffe, Tami, 138
Rattner, Matt, 158
Ritual's Perfect Pork Belly, 156
Ritual Tavern, 10, 156
Riviera Supper Club, 98
Roasted Apple Soup with Hoppy "Grilled Cheese," 25-26
Rock Bottom Brewery, 196
Rock Bottom Stout Cupcakes, 196
Rossman, Jeff, 88, 96, 110
Russian Imperial Beer Nog, 211

S

San Diego, 8-11
San Diego Brewing Co., 30
San Diego Crostini, 168
Searsucker, 9, 116, 185
Searsucker's Apple & Ale Muffins, 185
Searsucker's Cali Belgique Short Rib Sandwich, 116
Selis, Dan, 138
Selis, Sarah, 138

Segura, Paul, 145, 146
Schultz, Schuyler, 71
Sieminski, Brandon, 41, 100
Silva, Chuck, 64
Skubic, Michael, 80
Small Bar, 66
Small Bar's Beer-Batter Fish with Remoulade, 66
SOL Markets, 136, 171, 204
Soroko, Nate, 10, 17, 91, 166, 173, 175, 179, 191
Sour Wench-Braised Duck, 103
Spicy Curry with Crispy Pork Belly and Hop Oil, 114
Spicy IPA Burger, 131
Spicy-O-Life BBQ Basting or Dipping Sauce, 41
Steamed Black Cod, 71
Steele, Mitch, 10, 134
Stein Diego, 44
Stilton (cheese), 56, 57
Stockberger, Jason, 196
Stone Brewing Co., 10, 37, 40, 122, 134, 142, 211
Stone Brewing World Bistro & Gardens, 10, 37, 122
Stone Smoked Porter Chili, 134
Stone's Tilapia Ceviche, 37
Stout-Braised Pork Belly, 129-130
Studebaker, Ryan, 9, 92
Sweet Georgia Brown Lamb Stew, 152
Sysak, Bill ("Dr."), 11, 122, 142

T
Taste Cheese, 50
Tempeh Shepherd's Pie, 122
Three-Day Mission Amber Pork Belly, 124
Three Li'l Pigs Burger, 96
Tiger! Tiger!, 9, 94
Tiger! Tiger! Bratwurst, 94
Tondro, Grant, 113
Toronado, 10, 17, 91, 173, 191

Toronado's Arrabiata, 91
Toronado's Famous Fromage Fort, 17
Toronado's Stout Nutella Trifle, 191
Tracy, Jesse, 34
Travaskis, Jeff, 34
Trenchermen (The), 165

U
Upham, Charlie, 98
Urban Solace, 129
Urge Gastropub, 9, 113
Urge Gastropub's Sculpin Mac & Cheese, 113

V
Velvet Glove Mac 'n' Cheese, 100
Vine Cottage (The), 71

W
Wahoo Wheat Cioppino, 60
Warfield, A.G., 131, 132, 155
Warnke, Bill, 105
Wasabi Cole Slaw, 40
White, Jack, 14
White, Jennifer, 14, 15
White Labs, 43, 114

Z
Zien, Peter, 22

beer index

A

Anchor Steam, 66
Anvil ESB (AleSmith), 84
Arrogant Bastard (Stone), 186
Avant-Garde (Lost Abbey), 161
Avery IPA, 53
Aztec Amber, 126

B

Balboa Extra Pale Ale (San Diego Brewing), 30
Ballast Point Pale Ale, 38, 150
Ballast Point Guezue, 75
Barmy Ale (Ballast Point), 208
Big Barrel Double IPA (Karl Strauss), 145
Black Lightning Porter (Lightning), 155
Black Market Hefeweizen, 92
Black Marlin Porter (Ballast Point), 84, 179, 194
Blind Pig IPA, 53
Brother Levonian Saison (Ballast Point), 75

C

Cali Belgique (Stone), 82, 116
Calico Amber Ale (Ballast Point), 49, 50, 51
Cuvee de Tomme (Lost Abbey), 91

D

Dark Brut Brouwerj de Landtsheer (Malheur), 54
Double Barrel Ale (Firestone), 50, 51
Double Chocolate Stout (Young's), 55, 56, 118
Dubbel Fisted (Iron Fist), 63
Duchesse de Bourgogne (Verhaughe), 55, 56
Duvel, 71

E

1870 IPA (Julian Brewing), 53

E

Elemental Pilsner (Lightning), 66, 105
Endless Summer Light (Karl Strauss), 145

F

Fair Weather Pale Ale (Lightning), 105
Fullsuit Belgian Style Brown Ale (Karl Strauss), 147

G

Gillespie Brown (Manzanita), 185
Grand Cru (AleSmith), 188
Grazias (Hess), 80
Green Flash Barleywine, 64, 136
Green Flash Double Stout, 200
Green Flash Imperial IPA, 131, 186, 199
Green Flash Trippel, 64
Guezue (Ballast Point), 75

H

High Tide (Port), 131
Hired Hand (Iron Fist), 60, 82, 100
Hop Head Red (Green Flash), 98, 126
Horny Devil (AleSmith), 71

I

Idiot IPA (Coronado), 91, 131, 199
Islander IPA (Coronado), 91

J

Judgment Day (Lost Abbey), 63, 204

K

Karl Strauss Amber, 96, 145, 158

L

Lil' Devil (AleSmith), 18

Lost and Found Ale (Lost Abbey), 118

M

Mission Amber, 124, 138
Mission Blonde, 34
Mission Hefeweizen, 76, 92
Mongo (Port), 91, 114

N

Nautical Nut Brown (AleSmith), 98, 185
Navigator Dopplebock (Ballast Point), 186, 187
Nelson IPA (Alpine), 131, 199
New English Brewers Special Brown, 140, 156, 185
Night Shift Porter (Mother Earth), 203

O

O'Brien's IPA (Alpine), 53
Off the Rails (Karl Strauss), 147
Older Viscosity (Port), 200, 211
Old Guardian (Stone), 136
Old Numbskull Barleywine (AleSmith), 56, 57, 84, 136
Old Rasputin (North Coast), 211
Old Stock Ale (North Coast), 54, 55
Orange Ave. Wit (Coronado), 21, 76, 92
Orange Wheat (Hangar 24), 21, 92
Orval, 53, 71

P

Pineapple X-Press (Monkey Paw), 38
Pupil IPA (Societe), 44, 199
Pure Hoppiness (Alpine), 43, 199

R

Rayon Vert (Green Flash), 52, 53
Red Barn Ale (Lost Abbey), 32, 33, 82
Red Poppy (Lost Abbey), 91
Red Trolley Ale (Karl Strauss), 44, 147, 145, 158
Renegade Blonde (Iron Fist), 18, 34, 66, 100
Riverwalk Blonde (Manzanita), 34
Rodanbach, 91
Round About Chocolate Oatmeal Stout (Mother Earth), 182

Ruination IPA (Stone), 37, 114

S

Sacrifice Red IPA (Aztec), 98
Sculpin IPA (Ballast Point), 14, 29, 60, 113, 114, 176, 186, 199
Serpent Stout (Lost Abbey), 200
Shark Attack (Port), 126
Shipwrecked Double IPA (Mission), 78, 131
Silva Stout (Green Flash), 200
Sour Wench (Ballast Point), 75, 103, 173, 208
Speedway Stout (AleSmith), 84, 98, 155, 191, 192, 211
Spice of Life (Iron Fist), 21, 41, 100
St. Bernardus, 142
Stone IPA, 122, 131, 134
Stone Pale Ale, 134
Stone Imperial Russian Stout, 211
Stone Smoked Porter, 88, 110, 122, 134
Stoopid Stout (Coronado), 155
Summer San Salvador Saison (Ballast Point), 168
Sweet Georgia Brown (Monkey Paw), 152

T

Tower 10 IPA (Karl Strauss), 145, 158
Tower 20 IIPA (Karl Strauss), 145
Two Tortugas (Karl Strauss), 63
Thunderweizen (Lightning), 21, 60, 76
Trippel (Green Flash), 64

V

Velvet Glove (Iron Fist), 100, 155

W

Wahoo Wheat (Ballast Point), 60, 75, 171, 199
Wee Heavy (AleSmith), 22
West Coast IPA (Green Flash), 43, 91, 114, 199
Why ? Not (New English), 60, 76
Wreck Alley (Karl Strauss), 206

X

X (AleSmith), 18, 66